A Heart's Second Chance
Our Journey of Faith

"ॐ त्र्यम्बकं यजामहे सुगन्धिं पुष्टिवर्धनम्।
उर्वारुकमिव बन्धनान् मृत्योर्मुक्षीय मामृतात्॥ "

Saavantus Excellence

(www.saavantus.com)

Contents

Contents... iii

About the Authors vi

Dedication.. xi

Part-I A Heart's Second Chance: Our Journey of Faith................. 1

   1. Building Dreams Amidst the Rush of Life 1

   2. The Lockdown Announcement: Covid19 Impact................... 7

   3. The Toll of the Lockdown.................................... 11

   4. A Sudden Health Crisis.. 17

   5. The ICU and the Battle for Life 25

   6. The Tension Mounts.................................... 32

   7. The Sudden Fall Without Warning! 38

   8. Faith Prayer Healing..................................... 60

   9. The Decision to Act....................................... 68

   10. The Road to Recovery.................................. 75

   11. A Moment of Tradition 79

   12. The Positive Sign of Hope............................... 84

Part-II Epilogue: His Voice, My Faith 92

   1. Looking Back... 93

     Cardiac Arrest in Hospital 99

     Life After Cardiac Arrest............................ 103

     Back Home-Sweet Home 109

     The Early Days at Home 111

     Rebuilding Strength................................. 113

     The Role of Faith and Meditation.................... 114

     Physical Recovery and Lifestyle Changes 115

     Rediscovering Life.................................. 116

   2. The Hidden Load: Unpacking the IT Lifestyle 118

     Sedentary Work Life: Trapped in a Chair............. 119

     Stress and Deadlines: A Constant Mental Whiplash........ 120

     Irregular Eating Habits: Convenience Over Nutrition 121

     Lack of Physical Activity: Always Tomorrow.................. 122

Tech-Enabled Anxiety: Never Truly Disconnected 123

Urban Triggers in Bengaluru: A City at War 124

3. Silent Warnings: Biological and Emotional Factors 125

Constant Fatigue That Did Not Go Away 126

Frequent Indigestion and Chest Discomfort 127

Sleep Disturbances and Restlessness 128

Unacknowledged Anxiety and Mood Changes 129

Blood Pressure and Cholesterol: Hidden Numbers 130

Family History and Genetics: The Silent Companion 131

4. Reclaiming Health: A Blueprint for Prevention 132

Rethinking the Workday: Designing a Heart-Friendly Routine 133

Nutrition Reset: Fuel, Not Filler 134

Exercise as a Non-Negotiable 135

Stress Management: Breaking the Cycle 136

Regular Check-Ups: The Dashboard for Life 137

Digital Boundaries: Taking Back Control 139

Rediscovering Life Beyond Work 140

5. The Road Ahead: Living with Awareness and Intention 141

Awareness: The Quiet Power of Paying Attention 142

The Art of Saying 'No' 143

Healing the Mind: Therapy, Reflection, and Emotional Fitness 144

Embracing Slowness in a Fast World 144

Redefining Success 145

Community and Connection: Sharing Story 146

Living With Intention: A New Philosophy 146

6. Final Words: For Every IT Professional Out There 148

7. A Second Chance: A New Purpose 149

8. After the Fall: What We Learned 152

Health Not Optional 152

Never Ignore Symptoms 152

Family is your Greatest Strength 153

Faith as a Form of Medicine 153

Believe in God and The Power of Meditation *153*

Simplicity Underrated *154*

Physical Movement is Healing *154*

Stress A Silent Killer *154*

Laughter Therapeutic *155*

New life - New Habits *155*

Every Moment as a Blessing *155*

Part-III Five Beats to Heart Healing (5D): Data, Diagnostics, Diet, Devotion, Dedication *157*

1. The Mathematical Triggers: What the Data Reveals *158*

2. Predicting and Preventing with Data: Driven Diagnostics *166*

3. Healing Inside Out: The Power of Diet *174*

4. Beyond Science: The Power of Devotion *187*

5. Dedication from Friends and Support: Bound by Love *195*

Two Hundred Days Later *203*

Acknowledgments *204*

About the Authors

Mukesh Kumar Das is a seasoned IT professional with over 25 years of rich experience in infrastructure management, cloud computing, and program management. With deep expertise spanning leading-edge technologies such as AWS, Artificial Intelligence (AI), and automation, Mukesh has consistently stayed at the forefront of innovation. He holds a Master of Computer Applications (MCA) from NIT Raipur and a suite of prestigious certifications, including AWS Solution Architect, Azure, ITIL® Expert, and PMP®.

As an author, Mukesh has a passion for simplifying complex topics and empowering others through knowledge. His books *Cloud Migration: The Definitive Guide*, *Demystifying AWS: Unleash the Power of the Cloud*, and *Artificial Intelligence: In-Depth Introduction* have earned him recognition for their clarity, depth, and practical insights.

Beyond his professional accolades, Mukesh's life took an unexpected turn during the

COVID-19 pandemic when he suffered a major heart attack followed by two cardiac arrests. Through timely medical care, resilience, and sheer determination, he made a miraculous recovery. This life-altering experience gave him a renewed sense of purpose and inspired him to co-author this book with his wife. Together, they share a deep personal journey of survival, faith, and transformation.

Today, Mukesh is an advocate for heart health and work-life balance, encouraging professionals to prioritize their well-being. His story is not just about survival, it is about rediscovering life with gratitude, balance, and a commitment to making every moment count.

Bharti Das has added her debut work to a personal and powerful narrative inspired by real-life events. In her writing, she aims to bring awareness to heart health, caregiving challenges, and the healing power of faith.

Her calm and strength during her husband's critical health crisis became the foundation of this book. She believes in sharing live experiences to inspire, heal, and guide others who may face similar storms.

Together, Bharti and Mukesh share their story to inspire others to find faith, strength, and healing in the face of adversity.

Preface

In May 2020, during the height of the Covid 19 pandemic, our family's life changed forever. What began as an ordinary day quickly turned into a life-threatening medical emergency. My husband, a dedicated IT professional in his late 40s, suffered a severe heart attack followed by cardiac arrest twice. In a matter of hours, we found ourselves caught in a storm of uncertainty, fear, and anguish, all while the world outside was grappling with a global crisis.

This book is not a medical journal or a textbook on recovery. It is a deeply personal account, a testimony of resilience, faith, and the human spirit. Through each chapter, we have tried to capture the raw emotions, the prayers whispered in ICU corridors, the sleepless nights filled with fear, and the steady flicker of hope that never left our hearts.

A Heart's Second Chance: Our Journey of Faith is not only about surviving a health crisis it is about the invisible strength of a family, the tireless support of friends and medical professionals, and the power of belief in medicine, in community, and in God. As an IT professional and caregiver, I have experienced firsthand the emotional, physical, and spiritual toll that such a crisis can take. I have also witnessed small and large miracles that reminded me how precious life is, and how easily we overlook our health in the rush of modern life.

I hope this book offers comfort to anyone facing a similar battle. Whether you are a patient, a caregiver, a medical professional, or simply someone looking for inspiration, may these pages remind you that even in the darkest hours, healing is possible through love, through prayer, and through unwavering hope.

This story is our truth. We share it with humility and gratitude.

Dedication

This book is lovingly dedicated to **Dr. Magesh Balakrishnan**, Consultant Interventional Cardiologist at Manipal Hospital, Sarjapur Road, Bangalore. His extraordinary expertise, swift decision-making, and compassionate care were instrumental in saving Mukesh's life during the most critical hours.

Dr. Magesh's calm presence, clarity in communication, and tireless commitment not only brought hope during our darkest moments but also gave us a second chance at life and togetherness. We will forever remain indebted to him as a guardian angel who stood by us with strength, empathy, and unwavering support.

Part-I A Heart's Second Chance: Our Journey of Faith

1. Building Dreams Amidst the Rush of Life

I am writing this novel to share a struggle of my life that is both painful and precious. It is a story of love, fear, and unimaginable strength. Some moments in life leave a mark so deep that time cannot erase them. The year 2020 was when I faced uncertainty and instability in my life.

At that time, I was a mid-aged consultant, working as an IT professional, juggling the endless demands of a fast-paced career while nurturing the delicate balance of family life. My husband, an experienced IT professional in his late 40s, had devoted decades to his career, adapting to the ever-evolving world of technology with quiet determination and grace.

We had built a life together, one filled with dreams, hard work, laughter, and the comforting rhythm of happy days. But everything shifted in an instant, a sudden heart attack followed by cardiac arrest that shook the very foundation of our world. In that terrifying moment, the life we had so carefully built seemed to be shattered on the edge of the unknown.

This novel is my way of honoring that journey the fear, the prayers, the silent tears, and the strength we never knew we had. It is a story of how love can endure the fiercest storms, how faith can hold you together when everything else falls apart, and how even in the darkest hours, hope finds a way to shine through.

Our family consists of our son and daughter. Our son was pursuing a degree in Computer Science at a reputed college in Bangalore, while our daughter was focusing on her high school education. Despite our demanding work schedules, we make it a priority to support and spend quality time with them, ensuring they receive the encouragement they need in both academic and personal growth. We believe in fostering independence and critical thinking, and often engage in deep discussions about their goals, future careers, and personal development.

We live on Bangalore's Outer Ring Road, a preferred location for IT professionals due to its proximity to various tech companies. However, the heavy traffic congestion in this area makes commuting to work a daily struggle. Long hours spent in traffic, unpredictable road conditions, and ongoing metro construction only add to the frustration. My husband often plans his commute carefully, sometimes leaving early to avoid peak hours, but traffic remains a persistent challenge. The stress of long travel times often eats into personal time, making it difficult to find the right balance between work and home.

Another ongoing challenge we face is maintaining a work-life balance. The nature of our jobs often requires us to extend our working hours, making it essential to find time for personal well-being and family interactions. We ensure that weekends are set aside for relaxation and bonding with our children, whether it's exploring Bangalore's vibrant cafés, visiting nearby tourist spots, or simply enjoying a quiet evening at home. We also believe in the importance of mental and physical well-being, so we try to engage in activities like yoga, exercise, and occasional weekend get-together to unwind from the daily grind.

In addition to our work and family responsibilities, we are also actively involved in community engagements and social causes. My husband enjoys mentoring young professionals and offering mentoring on career growth, while I participate in initiatives that promote diversity and inclusion in the workplace. Giving back to society has always been an important aspect of our lives, and we strive to contribute in meaningful ways whenever possible.

Despite these challenges, he remains deeply committed to his profession. He finds fulfillment in mentoring young professionals, sharing insights, and keeping up with industry trends. He strongly believes in continuous learning and strives to balance his career with his responsibilities at home. His passion for technology and commitment to excellence inspire not just our family, but also those who work alongside him.

Looking ahead, he remains optimistic about the future. He understands that challenges will persist whether in commuting, balancing work, or managing family life, but he is determined to tackle them with resilience. As a family, we continue to support each other through all the ups and downs, creating a life that is fulfilling both professionally and personally. Through dedication, teamwork, and perseverance, we navigate the dynamic life of IT professionals in Bangalore, embracing each challenge as an opportunity for growth and success.

2. The Lockdown Announcement: Covid19 Impact

It was in March 2020 when the Indian government made the sudden announcement: a nationwide lockdown to control the spread of Covid19. The news hit like a thunderclap, and within moments, the world seemed to change. A sense of dread and uncertainty filled the air as people tried to process what this meant for their lives. The streets, once filled with the sounds of bustling traffic and chatter, became eerily quiet, as though the city itself was releasing its own breath. The usual hum of activity gave way to hushed whispers of fear. People rushed to stock up on groceries, medicines, and other essentials. Shelves in supermarkets were emptied within hours as everyone tried to prepare for the unknown. The fear of running out of supplies was palpable, and long lines formed outside stores, as anxious faces peeked out from behind masks.

There was a sense of unease everywhere. The pandemic was an invisible enemy, and no one knew who would be affected next, or how long the situation would last. The air was thick with anxiety and the uncertainty loomed like a storm cloud over everyone's heads. People were uncertain about what the future held, worried about their health, the health of their loved ones, and the state of the economy. The world, it seemed, was in a state of collective panic.

But amid the chaos and rising tension, I found myself feeling strangely calm. The idea of being confined indoors didn't seem as overwhelming to me as it did to others. My daily routine had already been largely centered around the house, my work, my responsibilities as a mother, as a wife managing the household. I had learned to embrace the rhythm of home life long before this crisis. So, when the lockdown was declared, I felt a sense of quiet reassurance, as though I was prepared for what was to come.

I tried to share this sense of calm with my husband. But no matter how much I reassured him, the anxiety seemed to seep into every corner of our house. I could see the stress in his eyes, the constant questions, and the lingering fear that hung in the air. It was as if the anxiety of the outside world had found its way into our home. My husband, typically a calm and rational man, found himself unable to cope with the fear and anxiety. He worried about everything in the future, our safety, the uncertainty of how long the lockdown would last. And no matter how much I tried to keep the peace, to remind everyone that we would be okay, the unease persisted.

It was a strange time. On the outside, everything seemed calm, but underneath, there was a tension that no one could shake off. As the days went by, I realized that my sense of calm was not just a comfort, but a source of strength for those around me. It was a challenge, though, to maintain that calmness when the world outside seemed to be collapsing.

3. The Toll of the Lockdown

As the pandemic raged outside, creating an atmosphere of fear and uncertainty, I found solace in a belief that provided me with strength. I strongly believed in God's supreme power, believing that he was ultimately in control of everything, even in the aftermath of this global crisis. Anxiety felt like an unnecessary burden, a distraction from the faith that was holding me together.

It was clear to me that regardless of how terrible the circumstances appeared to be, God's direction and protection would ultimately prevail.

However, not everyone in that pandemic shared the same sense of calm. My husband, like so many others, found it difficult to adjust to this new reality. The confinement of being locked inside in an indefinite period began to weigh heavily on him, pulling him into a state of restlessness. While I took solace in our home's protection and quiet, we wished for the liberty that was once ours. The simple act of stepping outside, even if it was just a quick walk or a trip to the shop, became something faraway in our subconscious.

Despite having all the essential supplies at hand through online apps, and the convenience of online deliveries making it easier to manage our daily needs, we were not at ease. The walls of our home, once a shelter, now felt like a barred enclosure to us. My husband's anxiety was compounded by the sense of helplessness that came with the situation an overwhelming feeling of being trapped without any control. He believed that a little outdoors or some quick shopping would somehow relieve the strain growing inside him, that a shift of environment, even if simply for a moment, would bring some relief from stress and anxiety. It was a daily fight between my calm faith in God's plan and his increasing irritation with the limits that we confronted.

As the days dragged on, it became clear that the situation was not improving. The world outside seemed to grow darker with each passing moment, and with it, the mental and physical well-being of everyone around us began to deteriorate. The lockdown had started as a necessary precaution, but its consequences were beginning to reveal themselves in more profound ways. The lack of exercise, fresh air, and outdoor activities had a noticeable impact on our health, and soon, it was no longer just the fear of the virus that we had to contend with, but the toll the lockdown was taking on our minds and bodies.

In our household, the effects of inactivity began to show in subtle yet concerning ways. We were all confined to the four walls of our home, and the usual rhythms of life morning walks, grocery trips, meeting friends had been replaced by a monotonous routine of office work from home, meals, and screen time. Without any outlet for physical activity, we all began to feel sluggish, our energy levels sinking. Even I could sense the difference. There was heaviness in the air, a sense of stagnation that seemed to cling to everything we did.

Health issues, once minor or infrequent, began to surface more regularly. Acidity became a daily concern, and gastric discomfort seemed to affect almost everyone in the family. Even more troubling, the comfort of being home all day led to unhealthy eating habits. We turned to snacks, sugary treats, and junk food to cope with the stress and boredom of the lockdown. Each day, he indulged more and more, as if food could fill the emptiness created by the lack of freedom and the constant anxiety of the unknown.

I, too, found myself slipping into patterns of unhealthy habits, though I tried my best to maintain some sense of order. I made efforts to cook nourishing meals, to keep the household running smoothly, and to find small moments of calm in the chaos. But as time went on, it became increasingly difficult to keep up the illusion of normalcy. The weight of the lockdown, the emotional toll of isolation, the fear of the virus, and the growing tension in the household began to erode the peace we had once enjoyed.

The mental and emotional effects of this confinement were far more insidious than I had imagined. It wasn't just the weight gain or the acidity that concerned me, but the deeper toll it was taking on our spirits. The stress of not knowing when or if life would return to normal was overwhelming. We all began to feel trapped not just physically, but mentally and emotionally. The longer the lockdown dragged on, the more difficult it became to escape the feeling of suffocation, as if the walls of our home were closing in on us.

Though I tried to stay focused on the positive trying to maintain a sense of balance and order I began to realize just how dangerous the mental toll of the lockdown could be. It wasn't just the physical health issues that concerned me, but the way this prolonged isolation slowly worn out our mental well-being, creating anxiety, frustration, and a deep sense of helplessness. The days felt endless, and I started to wonder how long we could all withstand this mental strain.

4. A Sudden Health Crisis

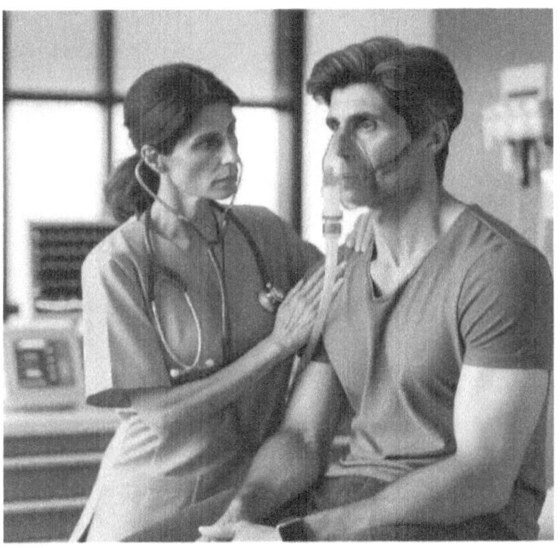

It was the night of 5th May 2020; everything suddenly took a sharp and frightening turn. My husband, who had been feeling unwell for a few days, started complaining of persistent nausea. At first, I thought it was just a passing discomfort, something that would resolve on its own. But as the hours passed, his condition worsened dramatically. He began experiencing severe vomiting and diarrhea, and the pain in his abdomen seemed to intensify with each passing minute. At first, we hesitated to go out to visit a nearby clinic due to lock down conditions outside though medical emergency was allowed on certain conditions. It was late, and the fear of venturing during the pandemic made us reluctant to go to the hospital. But as the situation grew increasingly alarming and his health continued to decline, I knew we had no choice.

In a state of panic, I booked an online appointment at the Manipal Hospital the very next morning on 6th May 2020, at 10:00 AM before the condition worsens. But he had another round of vomiting and diarrhea early in the morning accompanied by breathlessness after performing daily puja rituals in the home temple before we could connect with a doctor in our online appointment. He lay down on his bed though conscious and asked me to make a call and inform one of adjacent neighbors on another floor explaining the breathing problem issue. The friend reached our home in no time wearing a mask as new normal and then we made the decision to rush him to the nearest Manipal hospital in the morning 6th May 2020 at 09:00 AM. He was accompanied by his two neighbor friends to the hospital. The drive there was filled with silent, heavy anxiety, each minute feeling like an eternity. The doctors quickly began their assessments, and their faces, which had initially appeared routine, soon turned serious. Blood tests, ECGs (Electrocardiograph), and a series of other tests followed. It didn't take long for the doctors to discover the alarming truth: his heart was severely blocked, and his blood sugar levels had soared to dangerously high levels.

Doctor (serious): "Look, he's in a very critical serious."

Friend (firmly): "No, nothing is impossible or too critical. Please, just check him right away. He'll be okay. I have seen so many critical patients admitted and coming out of danger smiling"

Meanwhile, I broke the news to our family back in our native place about his sudden health crisis and that we had rushed him to the hospital for immediate treatment. Their reaction was instant shock, disbelief, and deep worry. Panic spread across the family as they struggled to process the news. Everyone was desperate to help, to be by our side, but the ongoing Covid 19 pandemic made it nearly impossible for them to make urgent travel plans. I could hear the helplessness in their voices as they pleaded with me to keep them informed every step of the way.

The other neighbor returned home after dropping him to hospital to pick me up to attend the hospital with all necessary documents and his medical insurance details. The news hit me like a ton of bricks. My knees went weak, and I could barely catch my breath as the words sank in. He had been hiding the severity of his symptoms for some time, trying to downplay his condition, but now it was undeniable. I felt as though the ground had been pulled from beneath me.

His health had deteriorated so quickly, and I hadn't seen it coming. There was no time to process the shock; everything was happening too fast.

The doctors explained that immediate intervention was necessary. When he admitted his sugar was very high that it was not measurable. He needed to be admitted to the ICU for further monitoring and treatment.

On 6th May 2020, at 10:00 AM, he was admitted with ST-segment elevation, indicating an acute anterior wall myocardial infarction (AWMI). He was intubated in the emergency room and immediately shifted to the catheterization lab. An intra-aortic balloon pump (IABP) was placed, followed by a successful percutaneous transluminal coronary angioplasty (PTCA) and stenting of the left anterior descending (LAD) artery. He was placed on vasopressor support to maintain blood pressure and circulation.

The stent process in the Cath lab will take around one and half hours they informed and as they wheeled him away to ICU (Intensive

Care Unit) after initial check-up, a wave of fear washed over me, threatening to crush my every thought. I was terrified of what was happening, of how quickly everything had spiraled out of control. But amidst the chaos and fear, I clung to one belief: that he would be okay. I prayed, held onto hope, and reminded myself that we had gotten through tough times before. This was just another battle we had to fight.

I informed all my family relatives about this health issue, and all were worried. The worry was that due to the pandemic it was difficult for them to travel and meet us immediately.

The hospital quickly became our new reality. The sterile smell of antiseptics, the endless beeping of machines, the frantic pace of medical staff all felt like a foreign world. And yet, there I was, navigating this new, frightening space, trying to keep it together for my husband, for myself, and for our family. I was in a state of shock, struggling to process the enormity of the situation.

As the hours stretched on, I couldn't help but feel that this was the beginning of a new chapter, a chapter I had not been prepared for. The world outside seemed so far away, so irrelevant in comparison to what we were facing inside those hospital walls. The pandemic, which had been so overwhelming in the background of our lives, now seemed like a cold concern. What mattered now was my husband's health, his survival, and the uncertainty that lay ahead.

This moment, this night, was the turning point I hadn't seen coming. The realization struck me hard: life, as we knew it, had changed forever. The pandemic had already altered the course of our lives in so many ways, but this was something even more extreme. The fragility of life had never felt so real. Everything we took for granted, our health, our routines, our sense of security could be taken away in the blink of an eye. And now, as I sat by his side in that hospital room, the weight of that truth was overwhelming.

Though I clung to hope, there was no denying the fear that gripped me. The road ahead was uncertain, and I knew that nothing would ever be the same again. Life had taken a sharp turn, and all we could do was brace ourselves for whatever came next.

5. The ICU and the Battle for Life

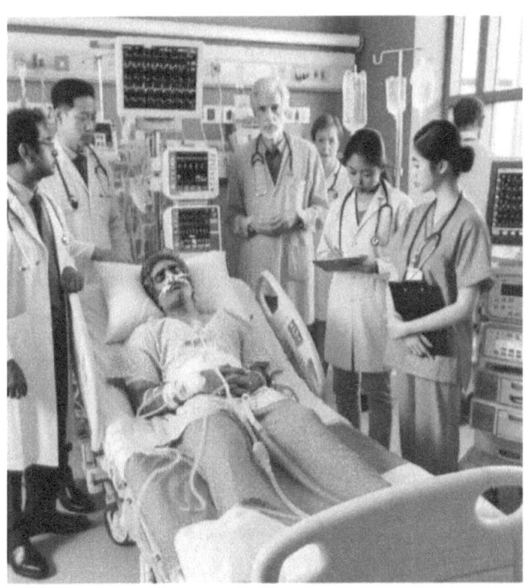

The doctors quickly assessed the situation, their faces grim as they delivered the news. My husband's condition was critical, and it became clear that immediate action was needed. His heart was severely blocked, and the only way to save him was through urgent surgery to clear the blockage. The weight of their words hung heavy in the air, and I could feel my heartbeat. Surgery so soon, so necessary, so uncertain? The reality of the situation was hitting me like a tidal wave.

Surgery started an hour after the hospital formalities were done and was successfully completed by 01:30 PM. The doctor came towards me to update my husband's health status.

Doctor: "The main blockage in his heart has been cleared, which is a big step forward."

Me: "That's a relief. Is everything clear now?" I anxiously asked.

Doctor: "There are still a few smaller blockages on the right side of the artery, but we're keeping a close eye on them. With the treatment and care he's receiving, we're hopeful he'll be okay."

Me: "What about other small blockages? How will they be cleared up? How is heart functioning?"

Doctor: "We're seeing some improvement in your husband's heart function. His ejection fraction has increased a bit, it's now around 30 to 35 percent."

Me: "Oh, that's good to hear. So, it's better than before?"

Doctor: "Yes, it's still considered low, but any improvement is a positive sign. We'll continue to monitor it closely for the next **72** hours."

During the chaos and anxiety, one thing was certain: due to the strict pandemic restrictions, only one family member was allowed to visit him to the ICU. There was no question in my mind whether I would stay with him. Kids cannot be at risk in staying at hospital due to Covid infection spread. As his spouse, it felt like the only right decision. I needed to be there for him, to offer whatever support I could, to help him feel less alone in this moment of fear and uncertainty. I tried to remain calm, but deep inside, I was drowning in a sea of emotions.

For the first time in my life, I was truly overwhelmed by uncertainty. I had always prided myself on being strong, practical, and able to handle whatever life threw at me. But now, in the sterile, cold atmosphere of the ICU, everything felt out of control. Every beep of the monitors, every shift in his condition sent waves of anxiety through me. I could not predict what would happen next, would not know whether he would make it through the surgery, or if he would suffer complications. I felt as though I was losing my grip on everything.

With every passing hour, I prayed. I prayed for strength, for power, for my husband's recovery. I whispered silent prayers, holding onto the belief that somehow, this would be okay. But the uncertainty of it all made it feel as though the weight of the world was pressing down on me. I knew my husband was in good hands, that the doctors were doing everything they could, but that didn't stop the fear from gnawing at me. The possibility of losing him was a thought I could not bear, yet it loomed over me constantly.

Next 72 hours were critical and meanwhile his condition continued to fluctuate, which only added to the stress and emotional strain.

One moment, he seemed stable enough to breathe a little easier, and the next, his vitals would spike, or he would slip into a state of discomfort. It was a constant rollercoaster of hope and despair. Physically, he was struggling with the aftermath of the heart blockage, but I soon realized that the battle wasn't just physical. He was also grappling with the psychological toll of being in the hospital during a global pandemic.

Every time I looked at him, I saw the weight of it all in his eyes. It wasn't just the pain from his heart's condition that wore him down it was the isolation, the fear, the overwhelming sense of being trapped in a place that felt more like a battleground than a place of healing. The pandemic made everything worse. Visitors were not allowed, and he couldn't see anyone else except me. The hospital, which should have been a place of care and comfort, felt like a lonely, alienating space. He was not only fighting for his life but also battling the mental strain of being separated from the outside world, from his family, and from the sense of normalcy that he had once known.

I could see in his face the frustration of being confined to a sterile room, the uncertainty of whether he would ever fully recover, and the weight of a world in crisis pressing down on him. It wasn't just the physical recovery he had to face; it was the mental strain of being during a global health emergency that everyone feared would never end.

As I visited ICU and stayed by his side, trying to reassure him, my own sense of calm was sometimes shaky. I knew that my presence was a comfort to him, but I also realized that I was trying to soothe my own fears by focusing on him. In a way, we were both grappling with our own battles. For him, it was the physical fight for his life; for me, it was the emotional turmoil of being in an uncertain, frightening situation that neither of us had ever experienced before. We were both prisoners of our circumstances, bound by the pandemic and its unyielding grip on our lives.

The seconds felt like minutes, the minutes felt like hours, the hours felt like days, the days like weeks. Every moment spent in that ICU room brought me closer to the understanding that this was not just a medical crisis. It was a test of endurance, of strength, and of the resilience of the human spirit. We were not just fighting illness, we were fighting the darkness that seemed to surround us, trying to find a way to hold onto hope in a time when hope seemed so fragile.

As the night stretched on, I continued to pray, to speak words of comfort to my husband, and to hope that somehow, we would both make it through this. I had to believe that we would, that he would heal, that life would return to some sense of normalcy. But at that moment, all I could do was hold his hand, watch over him, and wait for the storm to pass.

6. The Tension Mounts

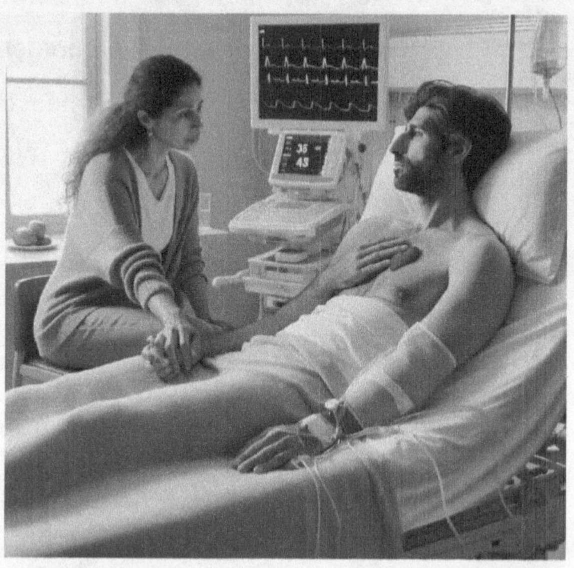

As the days passed, my husband's condition gradually improved, and the doctors reassured us that the surgery had been successful. He was moved out from ICU (Intensive Care Unit) in a hospital wardroom after four days on 10th May 2020, in the evening. His heart was stabilizing, and the immediate danger had passed. Yet, something about his behavior began to feel off. While physically he seemed to be recovering, mentally, he was not quite the same. He would become agitated over the smallest things questions about trivial matters that seemed out of place, worries about things that normally wouldn't have bothered him. He asked again and again about the kids, about how they were coping in Covid, and whether they were safe. His mind, I realized, was still under siege.

It was clear that the trauma of his illness, compounded by the stress of the pandemic and the hospital experience, had taken a toll on him. The fear and uncertainty had seeped into his thoughts, clouding his judgment and emotional state. His body may have been healing, but his mind was still trying to catch up, still wrestling with the aftermath of the frightening ordeal we had just gone through. The questions he asked, though seemingly harmless, reflected a deep-seated anxiety that I had not anticipated. He would fixate them on things that, before all of this, would never have caused him concern about how the house was being run in his absence, if the children were doing their schoolwork properly, or if I had enough support. It was as if he could not shake the feeling that something was wrong, something was out of his control.

As his wife, I understood. I knew that the physical trauma of the heart condition, combined with the emotional and mental strain of being in a hospital during a global crisis, was bound to affect him. The mind and body are deeply connected, and the body's suffering often triggers emotional and psychological pain. But even with that understanding, I could not help but feel the weight of the situation myself. His emotional state was not just a reflection of his own pain, it was affecting me too. I was managing so many roles at once. I was his caregiver, his emotional support, a mother to our children, and the one who held our family together through this difficult time. Each day felt like a battle not only for his recovery but for the preservation of our family's mental and emotional wellbeing.

I tried to reassure him, to calm his fears, but at times, it felt like no matter how much I gave, it was never enough. Every time I answered his questions or soothed his anxieties, there was another one waiting to take its place. And as much as I wanted to be the rock he needed, there were moments when I felt like I was crumbling under pressure. The emotional toll of this entire situation was becoming overwhelming. The fear of his health, the isolation of the pandemic, the uncertainty of what tomorrow would bring it was all building up inside me. Despite my best efforts to stay strong for both of us, I could feel my own reserves running low.

I could not escape the feeling that I was walking a fine line between caring for him and caring for myself. There were days when I felt like I was sinking, as if the weight of everything, the stress of the situation, the fear for his health, the constant emotional demands were too much to bear. But I had to keep going. For him... For our children... For our family... So, I did what I always did I pushed through, pretending that I had it all under control. I smiled when I felt like crying, reassured him when I was scared, and kept moving forward even when my own heart felt heavy.

What I had not anticipated was just how much the emotional strain of the entire ordeal would affect me. While he was grappling with physical recovery, I was carrying the emotional burden of it all. It felt like we were both trapped in a cycle of worry, fear, and uncertainty, each of us silently suffering in our own way. And while I tried to remain the pillar of strength, the truth was that I, too, was struggling to hold everything together.

The toll was evident in small ways: I was not sleeping well, consuming food just to survive not eating well. I was constantly on edge, and I found it harder and harder to focus on anything other than his wellbeing. I had moments where I felt overwhelmed, where I questioned whether I was doing enough, whether I could keep up the facade of strength. But no matter how difficult it got; I could not stop. I could not let my husband see how much I was hurting, how tired I was. I could not let our children see the cracks in my armor. So, I kept going, day after day, even when it felt like my spirit was starting to wear thin.

In the end, I knew that we were both going through a process, he **physically**, me **emotionally**. And though the weight of it all felt unbearable at times, I also knew that we were in this together. His recovery was not just about his heart; it was about all of us healing, finding our way back to some semblance of normalcy, and weathering this storm as a family. But it was going to take time, patience, and the courage to face the emotional aftermath of such a harrowing experience. And for now, I could only hope that we both had the strength to get through it.

7. The Sudden Fall Without Warning!

When my husband was moved from the ICU (Intensive Care Unit) to the wardroom, he was still exhausted and restless. He struggled to catch his breath, and I could see in his eyes something was not right. In the middle of the night, I called the nurse to check his pulse and blood pressure. She assured me everything was fine, but something told me his condition was not quite right. I could not shake the feeling that it all was not as it seemed.

The next morning, during the doctor's rounds, I made sure to mention my concerns. He reassured me that all the tests came back normal. "It's likely due to a blockage still present in the right artery," he explained. "We'll need to perform surgery to clear it in about **40 days**."

He went on to say that, for now, my husband could be discharged and that we would have to return for follow-up in a few weeks. The doctor seemed confident it was the best course of action, but I was not entirely convinced. Still, I decided to trust his judgment. I figured it was better to let him recover at home due to Covid pandemic spread, weak as he was, and address the remaining blockage when he was stronger.

My husband, eager to return home, was determined to prove to the doctor that he was fine. With a grin on his face, he walked confidently across the room, chatting and laughing, making sure to show off his strength. His energy seemed to surprise the doctor, who watched him with a mix of caution and approval. It was clear that my husband was ready to leave, his enthusiasm infectious as he reassured everyone that he was no longer the fragile patient they'd seen just days before. But inside, I could not help but worry if he was truly ready.

My husband was adamant about going home. Ever since the doctor's visit, he had been pushing me to get the discharge papers ready as soon as possible. His impatience grew with every passing hour, constantly asking me to hurry up. The hospital's medical insurance approval process, however, was taking longer than expected, and despite my best efforts, things were moving slowly. He urged me to go downstairs, telling me to speed things up, but there was nothing I could do. I could feel his frustration rising, but it was not helping. Finally, I gave in, lying back on the hospital bed as I was a patient, exhausted. He sat a little distance from me on the nearby sofa, his eyes fixed on the door, eager and restless, waiting for the moment when we could finally leave. His desire to go home was palpable, but I could not shake the unease that lingered, knowing he might not be ready just yet.

It was the evening around **3:00 PM on 12th May 2020**, when he was in hospital wardroom, I was preparing to handle hospital discharge process medical Insurance and paperwork. The hospital ward was quiet, my husband, who had been recovering steadily from his heart surgery, was lying on the sofa, flipping here and there. The mood in the minds was slightly lighter than it had been in days, and for the first time in a while, I thought we were finally beginning to move past the worst of it. The physiotherapist and the dietician all have given their instructions and prescriptions and how to take care of him after discharge from hospital. I was about to get the discharged summary papers.

But then..., **without warning, disaster attacked**.

AT **3:30 PM** I was in the same room staring him constantly, when I saw him suddenly falling from sofa with a loud sound. I saw him slump to the side; his face contorted in pain.

I ran out of the wardroom towards the immediate reception.

Me: Without a second thought. "Sister?" ...Sister, he collapses down from sofa please call the doctor, we need attention.

Sister: "What's wrong?".

Me: "He's collapsing...his heart again... Ohhh God, please. My husband fell... Please see him...Please call some doctor...fast...fast"

I could not watch him collapsing again and called all my relatives and friends one by one to inform one or other that something shocking happened again in the hospital wardroom the second time. I was not having strength to go back to the room.

Panic surged through me. My heart began to race as I listened to the announcement there asking doctors to reach immediately for an emergency. I could not watch the next step of action from the doctors but simply cry aloud outside of the ward near reception. I was not going inside thinking of any damaging unexpected thing that had happened to his life.

My hands trembled as I tried to hold my mobile steadily, calling everyone- family, friends and relatives.

Seconds felt like hours as I waited for the emergency response team to arrive. It felt like time itself had stopped. The minutes dragged on endlessly, irregular breathing and my frantic whispers of reassurance.

The fall without warning ...? Within what felt like forever but was only a matter of minutes, the nurses and doctors arrived. They rushed in, their faces masked and serious. Their movements were swift but controlled as they surrounded my husband, administering oxygen and connecting various machines to his body. I stood outside, helpless, and could not watch.

Me: "Is he going to be, okay?" I asked one of the nurses, my voice barely above a whisper, my hands still shaking.

Sister: "We're doing everything we can," she replied, her voice professional but kind. "His heart is racing, and his vitals are unstable. But we're going to stabilize him. Just stay calm."

My mind was a whirlwind of fear and questions, but I nodded, trying to hold onto the small shred of hope they had given me. As the doctors continued to work, "I stood frozen, swallowed by helplessness I couldn't fight". There was nothing I could do. All I could do was stand there and pray.

After what seemed like an eternity, the assigned cardiac doctor who had done surgery earlier approached me. His face was solemn, but his voice was steady. The doctor came out of the room after observing him towards me.

Doctor: "It was VT (Ventricular Tachycardia) and cardiac arrest in ward. We have given DC shock and high-quality CPR (Cardiopulmonary Resuscitation) was done. We've stabilized him for now. His condition is still critical. We need to keep him under close observation for at least 72 hours. There's a lot of strain on his heart right now, and we want to make sure it doesn't worsen. Second cardiac arrest had now worsened the situation."

Me: "I felt a wave of relief mixed with a deeper sense of dread. "But... he's going to be okay, right?"

Doctor: "We're doing everything we can. He needs to be shifted back to ICU and kept under observation. The next 72 hours will tell us more. Just stay close and be prepared."

The doctors and nurses stayed with us for another few hours, constantly monitoring his vitals and adjusting his treatment. He was sent to ICU again.

I messaged my kids at home, letting them know about his sudden heart deterioration and the urgent shift back to the ICU. Everything was happening so fast; it felt like the ground beneath me was slipping away. By the time the chaos settled a bit, I was completely drained physically, mentally, and emotionally.

Once he was taken back to the ICU, I returned home shortly after 5:00 PM to be revived. I had originally prepared for his discharge that day, packing all the essentials we would need to take him back home. But now, everything had changed. I asked the hospital attendant to call me if there were any updates, trying to stay composed, trying to believe it was just another temporary setback.

As I reached home and began resuming my routine tasks with heavy heart, the phone rang again only half an hour later, at **5:30 PM**. The hospital wanted us to return immediately. The doctor wished to speak with us and see my husband.

We rushed out in a car, driven by our kind neighbor. I tried to stay calm, but something inside me whispered that the news ahead might not be good. I heard from my friend that the chances of survival for him are less than expected. The drive was five minutes from home to the hospital, my heart was beating rapidly. That thought gnawed at my heart during the short five-minute drive back to the hospital. My pulse raced. Was this it? Was this the moment I had feared all along?

In my desperation, while on the way I messaged our mutual friend the astrologer asking him to look into the planetary alignments for that date. I needed reassurance. I needed hope.

Friend: "Don't worry. He will pull through. The planets show he is going through a tough phase, but this too shall pass."

Clicking to those words, I gathered what strength I could and prepared to face the doctor once more.

At the hospital, the doctor met me outside the ICU. His eyes held a strange seriousness.

Doctor: "Where are your kids?" he asked. "How old are they? They should come in and see their father."

A chill ran down my spine.

Me: "What happened, doctor?" I asked, my voice trembling. "Has something gone wrong?"

Doctor: "Please, just ask your children to see him," he said softly.

I nodded, heart breaking, a thousand fears crashing over me. Was this their way of letting us say goodbye?

Still, somewhere inside, I held on to my astrologer friend's words like a lifeline. I chose to believe him.

After that my children came to the hospital and spent some time with their father, they returned home. I stayed behind. I could not leave him alone.

As the night wore on, I was staying outside in the visiting area in the ICU. My heart was breaking. He was so pale, so fragile. I could not help but feel a wave of fear wash over me, an overwhelming sense that I was on the edge of losing him.

It was then that I realized how much I needed to lean on my faith, on the belief that God would see us through this. The thought was a fragile comfort in the face of such fear, but it was the only thing that steadied my trembling heart.

That night, I could not sleep. I sat on the sofa in the waiting area in ICU praying silently. My thoughts were a jumbled mess of fear, hope, and desperation. But through it all, one thing remained: I could not let him go. I wouldn't. Not yet.

In the stillness of that night 12th May 2020 I sat by his hospital bed, the beeping of machines the only sound breaking the silence. My heart was heavy, my hands trembling, and my thoughts spiraling into fear. I felt so helpless, like I was standing on the edge of something I could not control. The weight of uncertainty was crushing, and at that moment, all I could think of doing was reach out.

With tears welling in my eyes, I picked up my phone and opened our family, office and friends group chats. My fingers hovered over the keypad before I finally began to type through blurry vision. I didn't care about the time or whether they were asleep. I needed them. I needed their strength, their faith, their voices lifted in prayer.

"Please, pray for Mukesh," I wrote. **"His condition is critical. We need a miracle. Pray for healing. Pray for his strength. I believe in God's mercy, but tonight, I need your prayers to hold me up."**

Sending that message felt like releasing a piece of my soul, like crying out into the dark, hoping someone would answer. All I had left was hope and the power of prayer.

After I hit the send, I sat motionless, the glow of the screen still in my hand. Slowly, the replies began to trickle in first one, then another. Simple messages at first:

"We're praying."

"God is with you."

"Stay strong."

There are times when destiny seems to be against us, and no matter how hard we try, things don't fall into place. In those moments, I believe it's important to surrender ourselves to the supreme power and seek the collective strength of others' prayers. When all hope seems lost, faith and prayer can bring about a miraculous change. I experienced this firsthand during my husband's health crisis. The power of prayer, coupled with divine intervention, worked wonders in his recovery, proving that when we lean on faith and the kindness of others, healing can happen in the most unexpected ways.

But each one felt like a lifeline being thrown into the storm I was drowning in.

Tears slid down my cheeks, silent and steady. I wasn't alone anymore. Even if they couldn't be there physically, I could feel their presence holding space for me, holding hope for Mukesh.

I turned to look at him. He lay still, so still, a tangle of wires and quiet breath. I reached for his hand, warm but limp in mine. "They're all praying for you," I whispered, choking on the lump in my throat. "You're not alone. We're not alone."

The monitors continued their rhythmic song, indifferent to the ache in my chest. But at that moment, something shifted not outside, but within. I didn't give up. He has to fight and come back to take the responsibilities of home, family and kids. And if all I could do was sit there, hold his hand, and believe then that's exactly what I would do.

When I hit send, the weight of the request hanging heavily in the air, and I sat back, my heart torn between hope and fear. It was then that I whispered to myself, "God, please don't take him. Please don't take him from me."

In the darkest moments, when fear and uncertainty threatened to overwhelm me, I found myself seeking solace in something greater than myself: my faith. It was during this time of emotional and physical exhaustion that one of his close colleagues and friend guided one astrologer for guidance to review his planets. He suggested start preparation of chanting the *"Maha Mrityunjay Mantra"*, a revered and powerful prayer dedicated to Lord Shiva, believed to offer protection, healing, and strength. The mantra, which is often called the "Death Conquering Mantra," is said to bring peace and alleviate suffering. Sometimes in panic we are not able to listen to ourselves and forget everything, but there are people who support selflessly and remind us of the good things needed.

I clung to this hope like a lifeline. I thought in my mind that as soon as I return back home in the morning, I will make all puja arrangements to start this chanting in my home temple by lighting a lamp.

At midnight **13**[th] **May, 12:00** AM a patient attendant called me inside the ICU to acknowledge the critical situation as written by the doctor in daily hospital-maintained sheet.

They updated the current clinical condition, concerns regarding compromised cardiac status, heart rhythm disturbances, dyselectrolytemia, hypotension and need for stiff vasopressor support. They explained his critical status and possible risk to life. His heart was functioning ~15% only.

When I went inside the ICU room as suggested by one of our friends who asked to put sound of chanting of **the Maha Mrityunjay Mantra** in his ears once so that he can hear the mantra, I asked the attendant permission to do that and kept the mantra Jaap from my mobile near his ears. I was successful in doing so. Suddenly his eyes opened wide, and he struggled to wake up, but the attendant told me not to do that else if he is awake suddenly will not be good. After that I got scared and came out and myself was listening and prayed for him. But I was convinced that I had done my task to cure him.

The night passed in a haze of medical alarms, hushed voices, and the soft beeping of machines. But in my heart, I clung to the belief that God would not let him go. I had to believe that.

Even the doctor, I later found out, had not slept that night. The situation was critical, and the usual protocols did not help. Restlessly and deeply concerned, he reached out to his peers, consulted his seniors, and flipped through medical journals and reference books desperately searching for answers, for anything that might help stabilize him. I can only imagine the weight he must have felt. At some point, I think, a thought struck him... a glimmer of an idea that could possibly turn things around.

In Morning 13th May 2020, before 7:00 AM itself doctor visited ICU and met me for the next immediate action to save his life. It was quite early so no one was physically available that time to consent the doctor's decision so after detailed discussion with me and his brother in my native on a video call about the prognosis and the need of additional support to the heart **IABP** (intra-aortic balloon pump) device insertion started around 10:52 AM on 13th May 2020.

The IABP procedure is used to deliver blood to the heart when a blood vessel, especially near the coronary artery, is blocked. This procedure involves using a balloon catheter that has two lumens: one for gas exchange from the console to the balloon and another for guiding the catheter and monitoring aortic pressure.

This operation was completed around **12:49** PM successfully. As per the doctor, this is needed support to be given heart for that time of moment only and see what happens. This was a temporary solution in place to support the heart condition for at least 5 days. Meanwhile the doctor was looking for a permanent solution with his peer doctors and consultants in case the heart condition improves.

Around **7:06** PM the Doctor asked me to go for second opinion in case I want, and they gave me all details of management of him for second opinion. This meant that there are less chances of survival as per his current situation. Moreover, heart functioning deteriorated to 15% as compared to 25 % in previous attacks.

The IABP was supposed to be continued for five days. Meanwhile I was in touch with other esteemed hospitals and cardiac doctors referring to his report from the hospital.

But all doctors were of the same opinion and told them that this is a very critical case and what currently is going on is correct for him. We were not in a favorable position to move to another hospital as this hospital was near to our home, and it was Covid pandemic due to which I was reluctant to shift to another hospital in case its very much needed.

The next day, on 14th May 2020, was a blur of uncertainty, but each hour was a small victory. As the medical team continued their care, I held onto my faith and the love of those who were praying for us. And with every prayer, I too prayed for my husband's healing, for his strength, and for the miracle that we so desperately needed. The IABP support was now reduced to 1:2 as per the hospital-maintained sheet.

59

8. Faith Prayer Healing

"Let's do this together," I told my children, my voice shaking but determined. They looked up at me with a mix of confusion and trust, sensing the gravity of the situation. I could see the worry in their eyes, but I also saw their willingness to help, to hold on to whatever faith they could find.

Every day, as the evening light faded, I would gather my children by my side. Together, we would light a small oil lamp in the temple at home, a symbol of light in the midst of our darkness. The flickering flame seemed to represent the fragile thread of hope that we held on to, and as the warm light danced in the quiet room, I would lead them in chanting the mantra.

"ॐ त्र्यम्बकं यजामहे सुगन्धिं पुष्टिवर्धनम्।
उर्वारुकमिव बन्धनान् मृत्योर्मुक्षीय मामृतात्॥ "

"Om Tryambakam Yajamahe Sugandhim Pushtivardhanam /

Urvarukamiva Bandhanan Mrityor Mukshiya Maamritat // "

Our voices would resonate through the house, echoing our chants for healing, for strength, for protection. The mantra would become our daily rhythm, a constant reminder that despite the storm surrounding us, we had faith, we had hope, and we had each other. We cooked only Satvik food and vegetables in those days and stopped non-vegetarian food for all these days. I am now aware of how the speechless animals will experience when they are slaughtered and killed for our luxurious lifestyle. A slightly human torn heart or liver if damaged caused so much health damage, then what if we kill and consume animals? Every animal is entitled to live in this God created world.

The days blended long, quiet hours of waiting, of hoping, of praying. Each time we chanted, I felt a sense of peace. In the silence that followed, I would sit still, listening for any sign of improvement in my husband's condition. The constant beeping of the hospital machines and the sterile smell of antiseptic had become part of the backdrop of our lives. But in the temple at home surrounded by the warmth of the lamp and the sound of our voices in harmony, I found a momentary relief from the continuous worry.

The days passed slowly, but gradually, there were small signs of progress. My husband's condition, which had once seemed so precarious, began to stabilize. The doctors were cautiously optimistic, but there was no guarantee. I watched his vitals improve, his heart rate steadying, his breathing becoming less labored. Yet, the question remained: Would he survive this ordeal?

Even though his condition was no longer as critical, I couldn't shake the uncertainty that lingered in the air. Despite medical advancements, despite the prayers, I still feared the worst. Would he make it through? Would he recover fully, or was this just a temporary reprieve from a much greater danger? These questions weighed heavily on my heart, and there were nights when the fear would rise again, threatening to undo the hope I had tried so desperately to hold on to.

But through it all, one thing remained constant: our daily chanting of the **"Maha Mrityunjay Mantra"** Jaap through day and night in front of an akhund lit lamp. When I was in hospital, I put on headphones and listened to the mantra. At home my kids managed to play Jaap in front of the temple and take care of the lit lamp to add ghee in the lamp. It became more than simply a prayer; it became our anchor. It was the thread that held me together when everything else seemed fragile and uncertain. I began to truly believe that the mantra was guiding us, that somehow, it was helping to bring my husband back from the brink.

On 15th May 2020, 12:33 PM still he had intermittent Rhythm disturbances, suppressed by overdrive pacing and was still on IABP support and vasopressors.

15th May at 3:22 PM day as he was still on ventilator Doctor updated:

"His all the limbs are moving, making eye contact, Chest was clear. Vasopressor support was Slightly decreased compared to yesterday which is a good sign"

Each night, after the chanting, I would look at my husband, asleep and stabilized but still so weak, and I would pray once more: "Please, let him survive this. Please let him recover." I would clasp my hands together, close my eyes, and believe, with all my heart, that we were not alone in this fight.

During the same night I got a message from one of my office colleagues who checked with her friend who was a Distant healer in Germany about my husband's critical situation. She made a prayer for him and also sent me a prayer in her message and asked me to follow the same to repeat it a few times a day with full heart. My prayers for his fast recovery were like:

> *My prayers to his fast recovery. May the healing angels cover him and protect him under their feathers and heal him faster*
>
> *May the angels of health clear his arteries, lower his cholesterol and do every miraculous effort to bring him back to normal healthy life… blessings be with him. Amen*

The following day, I was pleasantly surprised to see the doctor's notes, which renewed my hope and strengthened my faith.
On 16th May 11:46 AM Doctor notes:

"Vasopressor support was decreased. IABP down to 1:3 with goal to remove later. He is awake and interactive on ventilator"

On same day later in the afternoon 12:46 PM the Doctor notes:

"IABP may be removed now."

The journey was far from over, but with each passing day, I felt a little more hopeful, a little more certain that my husband would make it through. And as I continued to chant, with my children by my side and the light of the lamp flickering in the prayer room, I found the strength to keep moving forward.

Today I took my kids to hospital following all the norms of Covid while going outside. My daughter stands at the ICU entrance, frozen. Her eyes fill with tears as she sees her father lying motionless, tubes and wires surrounding him. She slowly walks toward the bed, voice trembling as she speaks.

Daughter (softly): "Hello, Papa... it's me... Adina" (Her voice breaks) "I... I didn't think I'd have to see you like this."

Daughter (tearfully): "You've always been the strongest person I know. You never let anything slow you down, not even time. And now... you're here, fighting for every breath."

She pauses, looking at his still face.

Daughter: "How are you feeling? Get well soon..."

Mukesh: "Why you came outside home, it's Covid pandemic...everywhere, be careful"

Daughter: "We are ok...but I need you to come back, Papa."

Then she came out of the ICU room immediately, a little worried as she saw this first time.

9. The Decision to Act

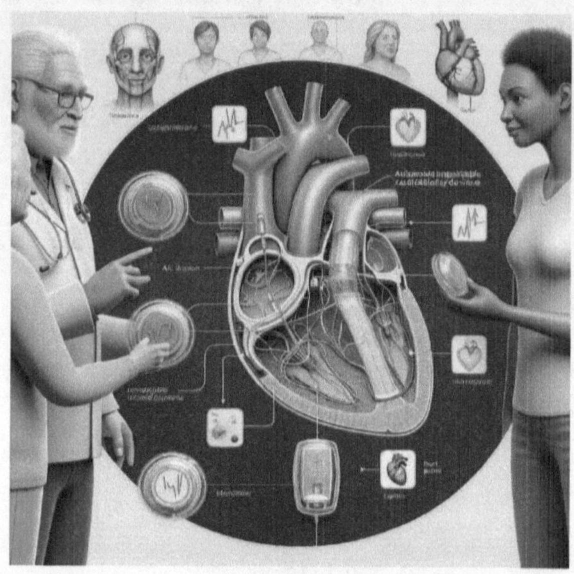

On 17th May 2020, 9:12 AM The Doctor discussed in detail with me and accompany friends the next options forward, risks and prognosis.

He discussed in detail the condition of him, prognosis, the need for **ACID (Automatic Implantable Cardioverter Defibrillator)** and risks and benefits of procedure were explained.

This was planned to be done on **18th May 2020** in the morning.

The doctors had given us a difficult choice. They recommended an advanced pacemaker known as an **Automatic Implantable Cardioverter Defibrillator** (AICD), a device that could regulate my husband's heart rhythm. It wasn't just a pacemaker it was designed to prevent life threatening arrhythmia by delivering shocks when necessary. The doctors explained that this procedure was critical considering the current working heart function at 25%; without it, my husband had a **50%** chance of experiencing another cardiac event. The risks of the surgery were undeniable. I could hear the seriousness in their voices; this wasn't just another procedure. It was a life-or-death decision (50:50).

I sat in the sterile hospital room, surrounded by medical jargon and the steady beeping of machines. I thought about the future what life would be like without him. My mind raced as I processed the information, torn between my growing fear and my unwavering faith. I knew how serious the situation was, but I also knew I could not make this decision alone. I needed to consult with my family.

As I stood in the room, my heart felt heavier than ever. Machines beeped around us, and a cold silence filled the space between words. I gathered the courage to ask the question that had been haunting me.

"Doctor," I said, my voice trembling, "what if... what if something goes wrong during the AICD device insertion? You mentioned there's only a 50% chance..."

The senior doctor looked at me gently, yet his eyes carried the weight of truth. He paused for a moment before replying, "Yes... there's a risk. The procedure carries about a 50% success rate in cases like this."

I swallowed hard, trying to hold back the tears. "And... if it doesn't work? What then?"

He sighed deeply, glancing at the rest of the team before continuing, "In that case, the only option left would be a **heart transplant**. But I must be honest with you, it's not an easy path. The waiting list is long, and matching donors are rare."

I felt the ground shift beneath me. A **heart transplant**? My thoughts were spinning. I nodded slowly, holding back the panic, knowing I had to stay strong for him.

I called my parents and in-laws, and even some close friends who had been with me throughout this ordeal. We discussed the options, weighed the risks, and agonized over the unknown. My heart ached as I listened to their concerns, and my mind was clouded with the weight of responsibility. However, despite their support and thoughtful advice, it was clear that the final decision would rest solely on my shoulders as everyone told me to take the decision on my own due to the risk of life.

The doctors said we could take him home now. "In case of an emergency," they assured, "you can bring him back, and we'll admit him again."

But how could I? How could I trust that I would get another chance another minute, another breath?

What if it happened again? What if he collapsed at home, and I did not have the time or strength to carry him to the hospital in time? I couldn't not shake the thought. My mind spiraled with fear.

We were still living under the long, dark shadow of the Covid pandemic. Hospital beds were scarce. Oxygen cylinders were in short supply. Ventilators were a luxury that not everyone could count on. I had seen people lose their loved ones just waiting in corridors waiting for help that never came.

I called a few **close** friends, my voice shaking as I explained the situation. One of my best friends then said quietly, "Who knows if we'll even get a bed next time, God forbid something happens again? Maybe it's safer to continue now while he still has the ventilator support."

Her words hit me hard. The utter truth.

"It's better to go ahead with the surgery now to have the AICD pacemaker implanted while he is still in the hospital. Maybe it could spare us the trauma of another emergency later… maybe even save his life when we least expect it."

Sitting there, trying to make sense of it all, I took a deep breath and prayed. I asked God for guidance, to show me the way. The moment was charged with uncertainty, but I found clarity in my heart. I trusted in God's will. This surgery, no matter how risky, seemed to be the only option that could give him a chance at life. I alone made the decision: We would move forward with the procedure.

On **May 18, 2020**, at 10:00 AM my husband was again wheeled into surgery. It started around 11:30 AM and completed by 2:00 PM.

The hours dragged by each second an eternity. I sat in the waiting room, praying, pacing, praying for some more. The uncertainty and fear weighed heavily on me, but I knew I had done what I felt was best for him. When the surgeon finally emerged with a smile, I felt a surge of relief. The surgery had been successful. His heart was stabilized, and the pacemaker was working as it should.

But the relief was short lived. The recovery wasn't immediate. It was grueling, a slow and difficult process. The road ahead was long, and I was about to find out just how challenging it would be.

10. The Road to Recovery

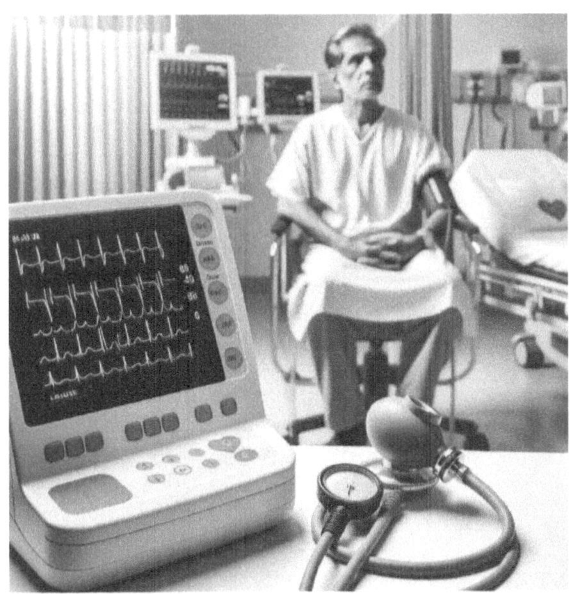

The next few days there was a blur of anxiety, exhaustion, and emotional strain. He remained in the **ICU** for constant observation, and I clung to the hope that each day would bring a little more improvement. But as the days passed, I realized that recovery wasn't going to be as easy or quick as I had hoped.

I spent few minutes by his side as due to pandemic visiting time was limited, watching as the doctors monitored his vital signs and adjusted his medications. I was learning how to become a nurse in my own right, how to check his blood pressure, his heart rate, his oxygen levels. I read through his medical charts, asking the nurses endless questions. I learned the names of the medications and how they interacted with his body. I was determined to do whatever I could to help him heal.

At the same time, the emotional toll was becoming unbearable. Watching my husband, once so strong and full of life, lying in that sterile hospital bed, vulnerable and weak, broke my heart. I could feel the weight of the responsibility on my shoulders. I was juggling the demands of caring for him with the needs of our children. They needed reassurance, attention, and stability. But how could I give them that when I, too, felt fragile? The stress and worry took a toll on my health as well. I had trouble sleeping, couldn't focus on anything for long, and even the simplest tasks felt like monumental efforts.

The emotional burden was further compounded by the isolation of the pandemic. With the strict hospital rules in place, I couldn't have any visitors. No friends or relatives could come to comfort us, to offer a moment of respite. I was alone in this. My heart ached for the support I longed for, but I was left to rely on my own strength and the strength of my faith.

The loneliness of the pandemic was all encompassing. My husband's condition had created a barrier that I couldn't cross, and the world outside felt distant and cold. I longed for the company of loved ones, for someone to tell me that everything would be okay. But the only thing I had was my faith and my resolve to keep pushing forward.

It was a constant battle of maintaining hope while facing the reality of the situation. I would pray every night, holding my husband's hand, asking God to heal him, to give us both the strength to endure. And each day, I would remind myself that no matter how difficult the road was, we had made it this far. We had come through the darkest days together, and I was determined to see him through to the light.

The road to recovery was not just about healing his body, it was about healing our spirits, navigating the depths of uncertainty, and learning how to embrace each day as it came.

Due to prolonged vasopressors support for 9-10 days his vocal cord had an issue then, he was not able to speak properly.

The doctor suggested to feed through renal tube. This was supposed to be continued for the next day, not sure how long.

11. A Moment of Tradition

On 21st May 2020, it was **Vat Savitri Amavasya** festival in Hindu's on the day when woman fast for long life of her Husband, I decided to perform the Vat Savitri Puja for my husband's wellbeing. I had always admired the faith of the women in our family who had fasted and prayed for the health and longevity of their husbands. But this time, I was doing it not out of tradition alone, but from the depths of my heart. For the first time in my life, I fasted for his health not with all the rituals as it was pandemic lock down and

I could not go out to buy certain puja items, but holding nothing but faith and hope in my spirit.

I gathered a few of the sacred items needed for the puja, and as the sun began to rise, I started the prayer with unwavering focus. Every prayer I uttered was a reflection of the turbulent journey we had been on. I felt the weight of those days, the sleepless nights, the moments of fear, and the emotional exhaustion. But in the quiet of that moment, with my children sitting quietly by my side, I knew that I was not alone.

As I offered my prayers, I reflected on how far we had come as a family. The pandemic had tested us in ways we had never imagined. The uncertainty of the world outside, the fear of the unknown, the restrictions on our freedom, all of it had taken a toll on our mental and physical health. But even amidst the turmoil, I had found strength in places I hadn't known existed. The lockdown had pushed us to our limits, but it also brought us closer together. We had learned to rely on each other, to lean into our faith, and to hold on to hope in the most challenging of circumstances.

Through all the fear and hardship, I had come to understand the true power of faith, prayer, and resilience. It wasn't just about surviving it was about finding a way to thrive, even in the darkest of times. And in that moment, as I completed the puja and prayed for my husband's recovery, I realized that these rituals weren't just about tradition. They were about binding us to something greater than ourselves, about bringing light into the shadows of our lives.

I reached hospital after performing puja at 7:30 AM early that morning. When the doctor called me to see him, I saw him and then bowed his feet and drank water.

Then the doctor visited.

Mukesh: "Doctor, do you think I could go home for a bit? If anything happens, I promise I'll come back immediately."

Doctor: "I understand your desire to go home, but given your recent second attack, I strongly advise against it. We need to keep you here for a few more days to ensure everything stabilizes."

Mukesh: "But I feel fine now. Is it necessary to stay?"

Doctor: "Yes, it is. Your condition is still quite delicate, and we don't want to take any unnecessary risks. Staying here allows us to monitor you closely and respond quickly if anything changes."

Me: "Doctor, I'm really worried after this second attack. I think it's best if he stays in the ICU under your and the nurses' vigilance. I don't want to take any chances."

Doctor: replied "I completely understand your concerns. Keeping him in the ICU is the safest option right now. We'll continue to monitor his condition closely and provide the necessary care to ensure his recovery."

Me: "Thank you for understanding. We'll do everything we can to make sure you get better soon."

12. The Positive Sign of Hope

I saw a bunch of lily flowers blooming in my garden on the balcony, one of the flowers I plucked and placed in my home temple. This flower is called Rhodophiala rosea, also known as Hippeastrum roseum, is a beautiful and rare flower with star shaped blooms that are typically light pinkish orange. These flowers gave me hope and courage to tackle the situation.

The days dragged on, each one a mix of hope and trepidation. My husband's recovery was far from easy. There were good days and bad days, but mostly it felt like we were stuck in a long, drawn-out struggle. Every time his condition seemed to improve; a setback would follow. Yet, through it all, I continued to stay by his side. I had taken on a larger role in his care, becoming not only his wife but also his caregiver, nurse, and advocate. The weight of responsibility was heavy, but I felt an inner strength I hadn't known before.

Then, on **25th May 2020**, after what felt like an eternity of waiting, the doctors gave us the news we had been praying for: My husband was ready to be discharged. The relief was palpable, but it came with its own set of challenges. I had learned so much about his care during his time in the hospital, but now it was time to transition that knowledge into managing his recovery at home. There were still countless tasks ahead with daily medications, regular checkups, and ensuring that he followed his strict health regimen.

He got discharged from hospital on 25th May 2020, in late evening.

The doctor has asked him to put a **Holter** machine in his body to monitor the vitals.

Holter's most common use is for monitoring ECG heart activity (electrocardiography or ECG). Its extended recording period is sometimes useful for observing occasional cardiac arrhythmias which would be difficult to identify in a shorter period.

The care was not just about administering his medications or ensuring he followed his diet, it was about being there for him emotionally, helping him navigate the mental and emotional toll of his recovery. The fear still lingered in his eyes. The physical pain was one thing, but the psychological strain of being in the hospital for so long, the isolation, and the ongoing uncertainty about the future were far harder to bear.

At home, I had also become more attuned to every aspect of his health. I was learning how to monitor his vital signs, tracking his heart rate, and ensuring that his blood pressure was stable. I adjusted my routine to accommodate his needs, waking up early at 5:00 AM to prepare his medications and making sure I was there for him every moment.

I was so tensed after getting back from hospital as was on trauma that the collapse could happen again, then what will I do alone.

I kept a nurse referred by hospital at home for 10-15 days to help me monitor his vitals and at the same time I can take care of his diet. Also, the nurse can monitor any unwanted health situation at home.

The mental and physical strain was starting to wear on me too. I often find myself exhausted, both physically and emotionally. There were moments of doubt, moments when I questioned whether we could keep going, but then I would look at my husband's progress, no matter how small, and remember that every step forward was a victory. The road was long, but we were moving forward.

I felt a sense of pride in how far we had come. We had made it through the darkest days together, and now we were taking the next step in our journey. I had learned to juggle so many roles wife, mother, nurse, caregiver and in doing so, I had discovered a strength I never knew I had. But the hardest part was still ahead. It wasn't just about getting him home, it was about rebuilding our lives, step by step, as a family.

This new chapter was daunting. The world outside had changed in ways we could never have imagined and so had we. But one thing was certain: We were together, and together, we would continue to face whatever challenges lay ahead.

In the weeks that followed, life gradually began to return to some semblance of normalcy, though it was a new kind of normal one shaped by the trauma of what we had been through. My husband's health continued to improve, though it was a slow and steady process. Every day felt like a small victory. He regained strength in increments, each one more significant than the last, and for the first time in what felt like forever, I allowed myself to feel a sense of cautious optimism. There were still moments of worry, but the constant presence of improvement reassured me. I held my breath through each step of his recovery, thankful that we were moving forward, but always aware that the road ahead would still take time.

Though many of our friends and family members couldn't physically be with us, their support was unwavering. The distance created by the pandemic had kept us apart in ways we hadn't expected, but I found solace in the messages, phone calls, and virtual meetings that flooded in. They reached out with words of encouragement, love, and prayers. It felt as though the whole world was holding us in their thoughts, even if they couldn't be there to lend a helping hand in person. I realized how vital the connections we have with others truly are, and how deeply they can impact on our emotional and mental wellbeing, even when separated by miles.

The experience of navigating the pandemic, my husband's health crisis, and everything that came with it had taught me profound lessons. I had learned to rely on something greater than myself, to surrender my fears to a higher power, and to trust that things would unfold as they were meant to. It taught me the value of love not just the romantic love I shared with my husband, but the unconditional love that emanates from family and friends who will stand by you no matter the circumstances. The love that supports you when you can't stand on your own.

Faith had also been my constant companion during the most challenging days. It gave me the courage to face each new obstacle, even when everything felt uncertain. I had prayed every night for my husband's recovery, for strength to endure, and for guidance in navigating the unknown. I had learned that prayer wasn't just about asking for help, it was about opening yourself up to receive strength from a higher place, trusting that it would always be there to sustain you.

Above all, I had learned the immeasurable value of resilience. The pandemic had shown me that resilience is not only about enduring hardship, but also about finding the strength to rebuild, to rise after your fall, and to stand tall in the face of adversity. As an individual, I had learned that resilience doesn't mean being unbreakable, but it's about the ability to bend without breaking, to adapt and grow. And as a family, we had embodied resilience in every sense of the word. The trials we faced had tested us, but they had also strengthened the bonds that held us together.

In the end, it was not just about surviving, the worst of it was about learning to thrive despite the odds. Through prayer, hard work, and an unwavering belief in the power of love, we had survived, and we were stronger for it. We had faced the darkest of times, but in the process, we had rediscovered our faith, our love, and the indomitable strength that resides within us all.

Part-II Epilogue: His Voice, My Faith

1. Looking Back

Hello, I am Bharti's husband Mukesh whose story was told through her eyes and heart in this book. Today, I want to share my perspective, not just as a patient who suffered a life-threatening heart attack, but as someone who has been profoundly changed by that experience.

Life often takes unexpected turns, and for me, that moment arrived in May 2020. It was a time when the world was already grappling with the fear and uncertainty of Covid 19, and little did I know that I was about to embark on a personal journey for survival.

I have lived through moments that hovered at the edge of death, and in doing so, I have emerged with a renewed understanding of life, love, and time itself. Looking back, the signs were always there. They whispered, not screamed. For about ten days before the heart attack, I had frequent bouts of nausea. There was a tightness in my chest that came and went. I even felt a kind of cold sweat more than once, often without any exertion. I chalked it up to acidity, to gas, to bad food. Like many men in their late 40s, I didn't want to believe something could be seriously wrong. So, I took an antacid tablet and went about my day.

Then came that night one I will never forget. It was on 5th May 2020, 10:00 PM after finishing dinner and was just starting to rewind. The chest pain came suddenly more intensely than before. It wasn't just discomfort it was like someone had dropped a heavy stone on my chest. I felt suffocated, drenched in sweat, and oddly cold. But I didn't want to worry about this with my wife. I said nothing. I tried to sleep. Tossed and turned all night, silently hoping it would pass but it didn't.

By the time morning came, I was in agony. At around 6:00 AM on 6th May, the pain was so severe I started vomiting. My breathing became labored, but I still managed to go through my routine, almost like a machine brushed my teeth, having a bath, even doing a short morning prayer. But internally, I was collapsing.

That's when Bharti stepped in. Her instinct, her observations, she knew something wasn't right. She told me she was booking a doctor's appointment immediately. I nodded, unable to speak much. Then I asked her to call my friend. When he arrived and saw me, he didn't waste a second.

"This is serious. We are going to the hospital. Now."

We rushed to Manipal Hospital, formerly Columbia Asia. By the time I arrived, I was visibly struggling. I told the nurse, "I think I'm having a heart attack."

From there, everything moved in fast forward. The doctors and nurses acted quickly. They examined my vitals, ran an ECG (Electrocardiogram), and immediately confirmed what I had feared was a heart attack. A serious one. The next thing I remember is being given oxygen, then hearing someone say, "He's critical. Prepare for surgery. We need to operate in Cath lab."

That was the last moment I remember clearly. The rest of it being sedated, going under anesthesia, getting attached to a ventilator is a black void.

I would later learn that not only did I suffer a major heart attack with 100% blockage in one of the arteries, but I also had to undergo an emergency angioplasty. A stent was placed to open the artery. The cardiologist later told my wife that had we waited another hour, it might have been too late.

I regained consciousness the next day. My throat was sore from the ventilator tube, and I was drowsy from the medication, but I remember seeing Bharti's face. She looked tired, her eyes swollen, but there was relief in them. I couldn't speak, but I nodded. I was alive.

When I woke up two days later, I found myself in the ICU. My body felt weak, and my mind was foggy. I soon learned that I had undergone an angioplasty to remove a 100% blockage. The procedure had saved my life, but my battle was far from over. After four days, I was moved to a private ward, where I was expected to continue my recovery. However, something still didn't feel right. I couldn't shake off a sense of unease.

On 12th May 2020 it was supposed to be the day I got discharged from the hospital. I had taken a proper bath that morning, feeling optimistic about finally going home. As the hospital staff processed my paperwork, I sat on the sofa in my room, waiting. And then, without warning, everything went dark.

At that moment, I had suffered cardiac arrest. Later, I learned that doctors and nurses rushed in, performing CPR (Cardiopulmonary Resuscitation) to revive me. It is an emergency lifesaving procedure performed when the heart stops beating. CPR combines chest compressions and rescue breaths to help maintain vital blood flow and oxygen to the brain and other organs until professional medical help arrives. I was immediately placed back in the ICU, connected to a ventilator, with the next 72 hours again deemed critical. My family, relatives and friends were informed of the severity of my condition, and all they could do was wait and hope.

For the next few days, I remained in a delicate state, but I fought through. Slowly, I started stabilizing, and after spending a total of 20 days in the hospital, mostly in the ICU (Intensive Care Unit), I was finally discharged. It was a frightening experience, one that changed my perspective on life forever. I had survived not just a heart attack but also a cardiac arrest. The journey was painful, but it reinforced one thing: life is *unpredictable*, and every moment we have is *precious*.

Looking back, I realized how close I had come to losing it all. But I was given a second chance, and for that, I remain forever grateful.

Cardiac Arrest in Hospital

After my angioplasty and initial stabilization in the ICU, I had begun to feel a little better, though the uneasiness still lingered. Breathing was slightly labored, and I could sense that my body was not yet in a state of comfort. But the staff was attentive the nurses monitored my vitals, administered the prescribed medications, and patiently adjusted the bed or position every time I needed it.

A couple of days later, I was slowly introduced to soft meals. I remember the feeling of eating again after surviving the critical hours it was strange but reassuring. After monitoring my progress and seeing my vitals improve, the doctors decided I could be shifted to a general recovery room. It was a shared space, with rotating staff and nurses checking in at intervals. My wife, Bharti, could now stay with me overnight, and a few of my close friends visited as well.

Despite the signs of improvement, something within me still didn't feel completely right. There was a subtle, gnawing discomfort a sense of not being fully "in the clear." I convinced myself it was probably just fatigue or the body's way of adjusting after a major procedure.

During this time, Bharti stated that there was another blockage the same doctor had observed but it cannot be treated immediately. "It's not serious for now," Doctor reassured me. We will take care of it once you've recovered fully, probably after 40 days when your heart gains a little more strength. I nodded, absorbing the information, and focused on regaining strength. I even started walking short distances with assistance. Each step felt like a milestone, and it gave me hope that I was close to going home.

A few days later, the doctor gave us the good news that if everything remained stable, I could be discharged the next day. We were relieved. It felt like the end of the storm.

On the morning of the planned discharge, I followed my daily routine. I took a warm bath, completed my prayers, and got ready with quiet anticipation. I even joked with Bharti that I was eager to get back home and have a normal cup of tea on our balcony.

I was also experiencing a bit of constipation that morning, which added to the discomfort. I strained a bit more than I should have, not knowing that this pressure might push my already strained heart over the edge.

By afternoon, Bharti was at the billing desk sorting out the medical insurance documents. I remained in the room, dressed, packed, and sat on the sofa, waiting. There was a sense of excitement that I would finally walk out of the hospital not as a patient, but as a survivor.

And then, everything changed.

I remember feeling dizzy at first. My vision blurred. My chest tightened like it had before, only this time it was sharper. I tried to call out, but my voice wouldn't form. I felt my balance give way, and in an instant, I collapsed from the sofa.

I suffered a cardiac arrest.

I don't remember what happened next. But I would later learn from my wife and the medical staff that a nurse heard the thud and immediately responded. The emergency team was called. The crash cart arrived. CPR was initiated. A defibrillator was used. I was revived on the floor of that hospital room, surrounded by a flurry of professionals fighting to bring me back.

Bharti was sitting on bed when she found me unconscious again, lifeless for a few terrifying minutes. "Not again," she had whispered, tears flooding her eyes. The same fear returned but so did the fight. And this time, too, the doctors didn't give up. I was brought back, stabilized, and shifted back to the ICU.

It was a blow to the hope we had built. But it was also a turning point.

The Cardiac arrest was likely caused by the unaddressed blockage combined with the strain from the morning. It was a reminder that even the smallest physical stressors can become fatal when the heart is healing.

Life After Cardiac Arrest

When I reflect on the time after my cardiac arrest, I can only describe it as a journey between worlds walking through a shadow and back into the light. Every second felt like a gift, yet the road to recovery was one of the hardest, most unpredictable paths I've ever walked. This chapter is my humble attempt to describe what life after a cardiac arrest truly looks like from the haze of waking up in the ICU, to the deep hunger for real food, to the sheer joy of seeing the sky again.

I later came to know that CPR saved my life. Cardiac arrest is different from a heart attack. It's an electrical failure in the heart, and without immediate CPR or defibrillation, survival chances drop dramatically. I was fortunate that the hospital team responded quickly. I was stabilized and moved back into the ICU, where my second life began.

That evening, still dazed, I heard a voice asking, "What is your name?"

It took time, but I remembered. I nodded and answered faintly. That small exchange was a lifeline it told me I was still here.

But as my senses returned, confusion also grew. I looked down and found two thick tubes inserted directly near my chest. I was surrounded by wires, tubes, machines. My arms were strapped; monitors beeped continuously. I couldn't speak. My throat was dry and sore. I tried to make sense of it all but quickly drifted back into unconsciousness.

In the days that followed, I was in and out of awareness. I could hear fragmented conversations, worried tones, medical jargon. At one point, I heard someone say, "His condition is critical. We'll monitor him closely for the next 72 hours." That statement registered somewhere deep inside me. I knew I was on the edge.

Then one morning perhaps three days after the arrest I heard a doctor say, "We've cleared the blockages, the balloon is functioning. He should start feeling better."

And I did. Slowly. Faintly. It was my second birth.

I began to make sense of the faces around me. The pain in my chest felt slightly less. My fingers twitched when I tried to move them. I could blink in response. It wasn't much, but it was the start of healing.

That's when I realized something strange: I was hungry. Despite being in the ICU, unable to eat or drink, my mind longed for food. I started smelling food when it passed through my room. The irony was cruel my body was fed through a nasal tube, and yet my nose registered the smell of roti, sabzi, and rice.

Every day, a dietitian came by to ask about my food preferences. "Soft food? Dal khichdi? Soup?" I would eagerly nod.

But no food arrived.

Instead, a nutrient rich liquid was sent through a nasal feeding pipe. I was nourished but not satisfied. I dreamt of warm meals, of family dinners, of festivals. One night, I was convinced that someone was throwing a party in the hospital. I imagined music, laughter, and a lavish buffet with biryani. I tried to get up from the bed and even attempted to remove the nasal tube. A nurse had to calm me and give me a sedative. I still smile at that memory it was both painful and humorous.

Meanwhile, strange sensations gripped me. My throat burned. Water trickled from my nose randomly. I couldn't speak. I couldn't move without assistance. But slowly, my mind returned fully to me.

Each morning, psychologists came by for orientation checks. "How many fingers?" "What's your name?" "Do you know where you are?" One day, I got them all right. My answer - "Three fingers. My name is... I'm in Manipal Hospital" - brought a tear to my eye.

The doctor smiled and said, "You're coming back."

Those words were more powerful than any medicine.

Gradually, the sedation tapered. The Central IV line (Intravenous lines) were reduced. The stitches from my AICD (Automated Implantable Cardioverter Defibrillator) surgery were removed gently. For the first time in weeks, I was free from Life Support machines, and restraints but the feeding tube was still there.

And then came the wheelchair.

A kind nurse asked me if I would like to sit near the window. My body was weak, but I nodded. She wheeled me down the quiet ICU corridor and parked me beside a wide window facing the Outer Ring Road.

That road was usually packed - honking cars, bikes, buses. But due to the Covid lockdown, it was eerily quiet. I watched the occasional car pass. I saw a bird taking a flight. I noticed a vendor pushing his cart alone. That was the first moment I felt truly alive again.

Sunlight hit my face. Wind brushed against my skin. After weeks of artificial light and sterile air, it was overwhelming. I cried.

The road to recovery was far from over.

Sitting up for a long time made me dizzy. Walking required the help of two attendants. Talking felt like climbing a mountain. But I had re-entered life.

In the days that followed, every small win mattered. Standing up for 30 seconds. Drinking warm water. Speaking a complete sentence. Listening to my favorite bhajan.

I also began reflecting deeply.

I had come within inches of death. Twice. And yet, here I was.

Bharti's presence throughout had been my anchor. Even when I was unconscious, I could feel her energy near me. Her prayers, her mantras, her touch those were as healing as the medicines.

I remember the day she brought our children on a video call. Their smiles, their hopeful eyes, reminded me what I was fighting for.

Eventually, I was discharged. The journey from the ICU to the main gate of the hospital felt surreal. Everyone cheered on- the nurses, doctors, and staff. "You made it," they said.

Yes, I had.

Back Home-Sweet Home

Coming back home after my cardiac arrest he felt like waking up from a nightmare except I was still fragile, still recovering, and still haunted by what had just happened. Yet, as I sat in the ambulance that drove me from the hospital to my apartment on the Outer Ring Road, I felt something shift inside me. The beeping of machines was behind me. The white walls of the ICU were a memory. I was alive, and I was going home.

My doctors were cautious. Given my history, they decided it was better not to shift me to the private room ward. Instead, they would discharge me directly from the ICU. It was an unusual decision, but one that turned out to be right. The memories of my collapse from the hospital sofa and the subsequent cardiac arrest were still fresh. I was vulnerable, emotionally and physically. Moving to a crowded ward with rotating staff, where response times might vary, could have been dangerous.

After several rounds of consultation, the date was finalized 25th May 2020. I would be discharged, but under careful home observation. A home nurse was appointed to assist me 24/7, particularly with medication, hygiene, and mobility. My doctors also insisted on installing remote health monitoring equipment. It would track my heart rate, oxygen saturation, and the vitals in real time. The data would be shared with the hospital dashboard every day for two weeks.

As the discharge hour approached, I was a bundle of nerves. I had come to associate safety with machines, with the vigilance of doctors and nurses. I wondered if my home, my sanctuary, would offer the same protection, but as soon as I entered our apartment, all doubts vanished.

The sight of my kids waiting at the door, the presence of my children holding a "Welcome Home, Papa" sign, the fragrance of freshly lit incense was overwhelming. I sat on the couch, finally back in the place where I belonged.

The Early Days at Home

The first few days were both comforting and challenging. I was still very weak. I could barely speak, as the nasal feeding tube was still in place. My throat burned, and I could not tolerate solid food. The nurse at home was gentle and efficient. She checked my temperature, oxygen levels, and administered my medicines with great care. The physiotherapist would visit once every two days to check my arms and leg movement. He suggested a few exercises be done at home. My progress was slow but steady.

One of the biggest struggles was adjusting to the Renal feeding tube. It was uncomfortable, constantly irritating my throat and nose. But it was essential. My body wasn't ready for solid food yet, and I understood that. In the meantime, I was given milk, protein shakes, and glucose through that pipe. I would often joke with my wife, "Even in the hospital, I got a better menu than this!"

Another interesting part of my routine was voice therapy. I had lost most of my vocal strength after the cardiac arrest and prolonged ventilator support. I was given a small breathing plastic device with balls that I had to inhale through slowly to rebuild my lung capacity. It was exhausting, but I was determined.

Fifteen days after my discharge, the doctor finally removed the Renal feeding tube. It felt like being born again. My first spoken words were soft, shaky, but emotional. I whispered, "I'm home," and everyone in the room had tears in their eyes.

Rebuilding Strength

Recovery was not just about survival. It was about regaining control of my life. The first month was all about learning basic functions such as sitting up, walking short distances, chewing food quickly, and speaking with clarity.

The food was bland boiled vegetables, oats, and egg whites. Oil was strictly off-limits, and sugar and salt reduced to bare traces. Yet to me, every bite felt like a triumph. I savored each spoonful as if it were a gourmet feast." The second month brought new milestones. I started walking again. Initially, I used a walker, taking ten steps at a time. Then fifteen. Then twenty. By the end of the second month, I could walk from one room to another without assistance.

But recovery was not just physical. Mentally I was still shaken by the incident. I had nightmares. I woke up sweating. The sound of an ambulance on TV or the smell of antiseptic triggered panic. My wife and I began journaling every night - writing down three good things that happened each day. It helped anchor our thoughts and allowed gratitude to flourish.

The Role of Faith and Meditation

One of the most transformative parts of my recovery journey was the role that faith played. Every Monday, I began chanting the **"Maha Mrityunjay Mantra"** - a powerful verse for healing and protection. I would light a diya, close my eyes, and immerse myself in the chant.

At first, I could only manage a few repetitions before getting tired. But gradually, I reached a point where I could chant the mantra 108 times every Monday. It gave me strength that no medicine could. It was not just spiritual, it was therapeutic.

Meditation became a daily ritual. Each morning, I sat in the corner of our prayer room, eyes closed, simply focusing on my breath. Inhale. Hold. Exhale. Slowly. Rhythmically. Purposefully.

I learned to control my thoughts, reduce my anxiety, and let go of the fear that had gripped me for months.

Physical Recovery and Lifestyle Changes

By the third month, my body was responding positively. My energy levels have improved. I could sit for longer, walk up to 3,000 steps a day, and even do 1 or 2 basic yoga asanas. I was particularly fond of shavasana (the corpse pose) - not just because it was relaxing, but because it reminded me of my survival.

By the fifth month, I was clocking 6,000 steps a day, maintaining a healthy diet, and sleeping through the night without interruptions. My daily schedule became a blend of spiritual practice, walking, light chores, and rest.

Our diet changed completely. My wife took charge of the kitchen, eliminating deep-fried food, excessive salt, and processed snacks. We shifted to whole grains, fresh vegetables, and heart-friendly oils. Every meal became a form of medicine.

Stress was another significant factor. I avoided work-related calls for months. We decluttered our home, switched off the TV more often, and played soothing music in the evenings. My family became my therapy group. We talked more, laughed more, and argued less.

Rediscovering Life

One evening, as I stood on our balcony and watched the sun setting over the empty Outer Ring Road, I felt a deep sense of peace. I had seen death twice and yet, here I was, surrounded by the sounds of birds, the aroma of dinner cooking, and the laughter of my children.

I rediscovered joy in the trivial things watering the plants, folding laundry, listening to my wife hum a tune in the kitchen. These were not chores. They were celebrations.

Eventually, I resumed working part-time. Just two hours a day, from home. My colleagues were supportive. My friends were amazed at my progress. But I knew the real credit belonged to Bharti and my children. They had been my warriors, my companions, and my healers.

2. The Hidden Load: Unpacking the IT Lifestyle

After the shock of the incident the heart attack, the cardiac arrest, the fragile moments in the ICU came the silence. And in that silence, I began to look back. Not just on that one catastrophic morning, but in the months and years that led up to it.

I had survived something most do not. But the real question was not just how he survived it was why it happened at all.

This chapter is not just about his life. It is about the life shared by thousands of middle-aged IT professionals across Bangalore and beyond. A lifestyle so common, so "normal," that its dangers remain dangerously invisible until it is too late.

Sedentary Work Life: Trapped in a Chair

For over two decades, my wife and I had built his career in the IT industry. I was diligent, sharp, and respected. But as the years went by, the work changed from creative problem solving to managing expectations, projects, and people. What did not change was the amount of time he spent in front of a screen.

Ten, sometimes twelve hours a day seated. Not a break to stretch, barely time for a slow meal. Laptop at chest height, shoulders hunched, neck forward, eyes fixed. Even during weekends, my posture rarely changes. If I was not on a call, I was still "available." The boundaries had blurred.

I was not lazy far from it. I simply did not have time to move. Meetings spilled into breaks. Small breaks skipped altogether. Days would end with fatigue, but none of it physically.

And so, over the years, my body became stiff. I moved less. And silently, dangerously, my heart adapted to a sedentary routine by losing its resilience.

Stress and Deadlines: A Constant Mental Whiplash

One of the hardest things to articulate to anyone outside the IT world is the intensity of mental stress. For me, it was not just about writing code or managing teams. It was about juggling multiple roles - leader, contributor, mentor, and people management.

Every new project brought with it a fresh mountain of deadlines. Client calls at odd hours, urgent fixes over weekends, and late night escalations were part of his daily rhythm. There was always something "critical" on the line. And even though there was not, the anticipation that something could go wrong kept his nerves wired.

I remember nights when I walked out of the bedroom at 2:00 AM, not because I could not sleep, but because I had to join a bridge call meeting. I remember Sundays when I kept one ear on the family and the other on my phone, waiting for alerts.

I carried stress not on his face, but in my heartbeat. Quiet. Relentless.

Irregular Eating Habits: Convenience Over Nutrition

Food, once a source of joy and connection, became mechanical. Breakfast was rare, usually just coffee. Lunches were sandwiched between meetings or postponed altogether. Dinner often happens past 10:00 PM, and almost always in front of a screen.

It was not that I did not know better. I did. We both did. But in the chaos of delivery timelines, stakeholder presentations, and urgent bug fixes, food took a backseat. Food will be ordered in, reheated, and eaten quickly whatever could save time.

The vegetables were sparse. Fruits, even more so. Hydration? Negligible.

And with every skipped meal and packet of fried snacks, his metabolism grew more erratic. My body responded with acidity, bloating, fatigue signals we brushed off as minor discomforts, never as warnings.

Lack of Physical Activity: Always Tomorrow

Like many others, I had a gym membership. And like many others, I rarely used it.

I promised myself to start walking in the morning. But meetings started early.

I planned to stretch in the evening. But traffic, calls, and fatigue took over.

Weekends, theoretically free, were often claimed by office work or errands pushed from the weekday overload.

There was always a reason to postpone exercise. Always a reason that felt valid in the moment. But the cost accumulated quietly.

My legs ached after short walks. My stamina declined. But I was too tired to fix the tiredness. That is the paradox of burnout, it drains your ability to recover.

Tech-Enabled Anxiety: Never Truly Disconnected

Technology was supposed to make life easier. But in truth, it made everything constant.

Slack messages arrived before breakfast. Microsoft Teams reminders blinked during lunch. WhatsApp groups buzzed after dinner. PagerDuty alerts didn't care about time zones.

Even when we were physically together, a part of me was always somewhere else engaged with a screen, responding to a notification, checking a dashboard.

It was never ending.

We normalized this hyper-connectivity. It became acceptable, even admirable. "I would always available," people said. But the price was invisible: elevated cortisol levels, disturbed sleep, perpetual anxiety. A mind that could never rest, in a body that was breaking down.

Urban Triggers in Bengaluru: A City at War

And then there was the city Bengaluru.

Beautiful in memory, chaotic in reality. What used to be a city of gardens had turned into a city of gridlocks and glass towers.

Even simple things like morning walk required planning. Traffic jams made commutes longer and stress higher. Air pollution from unregulated construction irritated lungs and discouraged outdoor activity. Parks were few and far between. Green spaces were often unreachable without battling through noise and pollution.

The environment outside reflected the pressure inside. Fast. Crowded. Noisy. Unforgiving.

Even when we wanted to do better breathe cleaner air, take mindful walks, reduce screen time the city seemed to push us back into survival mode.

3. Silent Warnings: Biological and Emotional Factors

If only we had known what to look for.

If only we had paused long enough to listen.

The body, as we would come to understand, rarely fails without first sending sign whispers before it screams. But in the hurried rhythm of our lives, I, like many in my profession, had learned to overlook these whispers. Tiredness was common. Sleepless nights were normal. Chest discomfort? Just acidity.

But they weren't normal. They were **silent warnings** subtle flags raised by a body under siege.

This section dives deep into those biological and emotional signals. It explores how long term stress, physiological changes, and even suppressed emotions quietly built the storm that led to that nearly fatal day.

Constant Fatigue That Did Not Go Away

It started small. I would mention feeling "tired" even after a full night's rest. We both blamed age. Work pressure. Sleep disorder. But over time, the fatigue changed.

I would wake up feeling heavy like his body was dragging itself through molasses. Simple tasks like climbing stairs began leaving him slightly breathless. Not alarmingly so, just... off.

I dismissed it. We both did. "You're just out of shape," I would joke. But it was not that simple.

The heart, when strained, stops being efficient. Oxygen does not circulate as well. Muscles tire easily. And fatigue, once occasional, becomes constant.

That was the first red flag. We missed it.

Frequent Indigestion and Chest Discomfort

I often complained about gas and acidity. Heavy lunches during long meetings, late night dinners, and erratic eating patterns made it worse.

I would keep an antacid on my desk always.

Sometimes, after eating, I would feel a strange tightness in my upper chest. Not pain exactly just discomfort. I would rub my chest absentmindedly and say, "It's gas."

And again, we accepted that.

What we did not know then is that many hearts related symptoms **masquerade as digestive issues**, especially in men. What feels like indigestion can be reduced blood flow. What we call gas can be a sign of cardiac distress.

That was the second red flag. We shrugged it off.

Sleep Disturbances and Restlessness

Another slow change crept in is my sleep.

I used to sleep deeply, rarely waking once I hit the pillow. But over the last couple of years, that has changed. I began tossing and turning. I would wake up around 3 or 4 AM, either checking my phone or just lying awake with an overactive mind.

I looked tired in the morning, but we chalked it up to "too many screens." I would scroll through news or LinkedIn, mindlessly feeding his insomnia.

But insomnia, in the absence of emotional triggers, can also be **biologically rooted** linked to stress hormones like cortisol and adrenaline.

An overworked heart often signals distress through disturbed sleep, shallow breathing, and nighttime restlessness.

We did not connect the dots.

Unacknowledged Anxiety and Mood Changes

I was not someone to easily express emotion.

I was calm outside. Composed. Responsible. Steady.

But beneath that calm was a growing current of anxiety.

In the months before my cardiac episode, I noticed subtle changes. I became irritable, impatient, and unusually quiet. I would zone out during conversations. My laugh was less frequent. I was easily startled by sudden sounds.

I told my wife, once, that I felt like my mind was never quiet. That even when nothing was happening, I felt tense like waiting for a crisis.

That tension, we would learn, was not in my head, it was in my body. Long term, **unprocessed stress does not just affect mood, it chemically reshapes our body's response systems**. Elevated cholesterol. Increased heart rate. Blood pressure fluctuates. Chronic inflammation.

My emotional shifts were not personality changes. They were physiological indicators.

Blood Pressure and Cholesterol: Hidden Numbers

I had skipped his annual health checkup twice.

Why? Because I felt "mostly fine." And when you are busy managing teams, projects, and global clients, blood tests take the backseat.

But when we finally did get him assessed after a little pushing his cholesterol was high. LDL value was elevated. HDL was lower than optimal. My triglycerides were not terrible, but they were not great either. And my blood pressure? It hovered close to the hypertensive threshold.

No medication was prescribed at the time. Just lifestyle advice: better diet, more exercise.

We took it lightly. So did my wife.

In retrospect, these were not "mild" deviations. They were **data backed warnings**.

My heart was underload. The vessels were

narrowing. His blood was thickening. A heart attack was not a possibility; it was a timeline.

Family History and Genetics: The Silent Companion

Unlike many others, I did not have a family history of heart disease. No bypass surgeries, no strokes, no sudden cardiac deaths in his lineage. In fact, on paper, his genetics seemed like a blessing clean slate.

But even without hereditary baggage, risk has a way of creeping in through lifestyle choices.

I was a **mild smoker,** not a pack-a-day habit, but enough. A few cigarettes here and there during long nights of work, or after a stressful meeting, or sometimes just out of routine. It felt harmless. Casual.

But the truth is, **you do not need family history to have heart disease**. Smoking even in moderation can damage blood vessels, lower oxygen levels, and harden arteries over time. The body does not grade on a curve. It reacts to every puff, every stimulant, every prolonged stress cycle. In his case, the lack of hereditary risk did not offer immunity. Because lifestyle had drafted its own story one that was unfolding silently, dangerously. We thought we were safe. We were not.

4. Reclaiming Health: A Blueprint for Prevention

After the storm passed, and after the doctors stabilized him and the ICU alarms finally fell silent, I and my wife sat together, overwhelmed by the weight of one pressing question:

"What now?"

We were thankful for a second chance. But second chances come with responsibility to not repeat the same patterns, to not walk the same path that almost cost us everything.

This topic is not about medical miracles. It is about the choices we make each day small, intentional actions taken by individuals that, over time, build a life where the heart is cared for, not compromised. "Because for every IT tech professional buried under deadlines, drowning in emails, or stuck in Bangalore's endless traffic - there's a way out. A blueprint to regain control. And it begins with awareness, followed by action.

Rethinking the Workday: Designing a Heart-Friendly Routine

The problem was not working. It was how work took over everything else.

We began by mapping a **new routine** not just for recovery, but for long-term sustainability.

- **Active Mornings**: We stopped snoozing alarms and began the day with movement. Not high-intensity workouts, just 20 minutes of stretching, a walk, or yoga.

- **Structured Breaks**: Instead of back to back meetings, we built in five minute screen breaks every hour. Stand. Walk. Breathe.
- **Boundary Hours**: No work after 7:30 PM. No work on Sundays. Hard stops became sacred.

The body does not care about your code deployment timeline. But it will show you when it has had enough unless you change how you live.

Nutrition Reset: Fuel, Not Filler

Before the incident, the meals were chaotic, skipped breakfast, takeout lunches, and late night dinners.

Afterward, everything changed because it had to change:

- **Meal Prepping**: We planned meals over the weekend. Cooked simple, fresh food. Balanced proteins, whole grains, and greens.

- **Timed Eating**: Dinner before 8:00 PM. No mindless snacking post-midnight. Eating in an interval of 4 hours.
- **Less Sugar, Less Salt:** Hidden salt in processed food, sugar in tea or coffee. We began reading labels and making mindful switches.
- **No crash diets:** No extreme fads, just consistent, thoughtful nourishment.

Exercise as a Non-Negotiable

We always said, "We'll start from next Monday." But Monday never came until we started.

Post recovery, walking became the first medicine. 15 minutes around the apartment complex. Then 30 minutes. Then 45 minutes.

- **Daily Walks**: Rain or shine. A habit, not a hobby.
- **Strength and Mobility**: Two days a week of light strength training, supervised initially.
- **Tracking Progress**: A simple smartwatch. Steps. Heart rate. Nothing fancy, just feedback.

I did not turn into a fitness influencer. But I became **consistent,** and consistency heals what intensity cannot.

Stress Management: Breaking the Cycle

Stress did not go away. But how he **responded** to it did.

We implemented conscious practices to break the cycle of fight or flight.

- **Breathwork and Meditation**: even five minutes of deep breathing changed his heart rate variability and calmed his nervous system.

- **Journaling**: every night, five lines on what went well and what felt hard. A way to release pressure.

- **Saying No**: I started declining extra work, especially during weekends. Prioritizing peace over performance.

- **Chanting 'OM'**: I started a deeply healing mantra to recite for five to 10 minutes to center the mind and support healing during health challenges.

OM (spelled **AUM)** mantra is considered the primordial sound of the universe. It symbolizes:

A (Ah) - the waking state.

U (Oo) - the dream state.

M (Mmmm) - the deep sleep state.

Silence after M - the state of pure consciousness.

Mental wellness is not optional because where the mind works as an engine, it deserves fuel and rest.

Regular Check-Ups: The Dashboard for Life

What gets measured, gets managed.

No more skipping health checks. Every six months, like clockwork:

- Lipid profile
- Blood pressure
- ECG and heart echo (echocardiogram)
- HbA1c (because borderline diabetes had also crept up silently)
- TSH (Thyroid Stimulating Hormone)

- Free T3 (Triiodothyronine)

We created a shared digital health folder which was accessible and regularly updated, reviewed. My body became **a monitored system**, not an ignored one.

And when you see the numbers, you feel in control again.

Mindful Steps Toward a Smoke-Free Life

I smoke occasionally for years. Always in control, never addicted or so we thought, but after the cardiac arrest, it was not a casual choice anymore. It was a **threat**. Quitting was not easy. But here is what worked:

- **Replacing the Habit**: Every time I felt the urge, I replaced it with chewing a clove, sipping water, or walking.
- **Accountability**: I spoke about it openly. Tracked the progress and celebrated the first thirty days, then sixty, then one hundred.

- **Professional Support**: I consulted a cessation coach once to strategize behaviorally, not just medically.

Today, I have not touched cigarettes in the last five years. My lungs thank me every morning.

Digital Boundaries: Taking Back Control

The IT tech industry never sleeps, but the human brain must not ignore its natural rhythm.

Slack, Teams, emails, Jira the endless pings, always created anxiety.

We took radical steps:

- Notifications switched OFF after 6:00 PM.
- Mobile phones are out of the bedroom, switching off the internet and Wi-Fi before bed.
- On screen free hour every evening.
- Stop watching the breaking news on OTT (like Netflix, Amazon Prime Video, Disney+, etc.) that are delivered

directly to viewers via the internet, bypassing traditional cable, broadcast, or satellite television platforms) and Television channels.

Initially, it felt like withdrawal. But slowly, we reclaimed **mental space** and with it, better sleep, better connection, better rest.

Rediscovering Life Beyond Work

Survival changed everything. It made us ask: For what do we live?

We began adding back joy:

- **Weekend drives without a laptop.**
- **Cooking together.**
- **Reconnecting with old family friends.**
- **Joining a local community health walk group.**

Cardiac recovery was not just about stents and ECGs. It was about purpose... Meaning ...Breath... Sunlight... Laughter.

We remembered what it felt like to live, not just function.

5. The Road Ahead: Living with Awareness and Intention

The night I came back home from the hospital, everything looked the same the study table where I once worked past midnight, the clothes in my wardrobe. But *we* have changed.

I was no longer just a mid-aged IT professional from Bengaluru juggling meetings and modules. I had become a **survivor**, carrying inside him a message one never gets to deliver:

"You do not get infinite warnings. Sometimes, the body speaks only once."

This section is about that message. About how we moved from fear to awareness, from survival to **intentional living**. Because a second chance means little unless you build a new road from it.

Awareness: The Quiet Power of Paying Attention

Awareness is where everything starts.
We became more attentive - not just to heart rates and test results, but to **emotions**, **environments**, and **energy**.

- When stress spiked during work calls, he noticed his breathing.
- When fatigue returned mid-week, we reviewed his sleep quality.
- When irritability crept in, we paused to ask: "What is out of balance?"

This kind of awareness does not come from smart gadgets. It comes from listening to the body, the mind, and the little signs we once ignored.

Awareness is preventative care in its purest form.

The Art of Saying 'No'

In the IT world, "Yes" is currency. Yes, to stretch projects. Yes, to weekend deployments. Yes, to after-hours "quick syncs."

But after the post-recovery, we realized:

Every 'yes' to work was a 'no' to health.

So, I started saying **"no."** Politely. Firmly. Repeatedly.

- "No, I won't be available post 6:00 PM."
- "No, I can't join another initiative right now."
- "No, I'm prioritizing personal time this weekend."

At first, it felt like a rebellion. But slowly, it became **liberation**. And surprisingly, work still respected him.

When you draw boundaries, you teach people how to treat you and how you treat yourself.

Healing the Mind: Therapy, Reflection, and Emotional Fitness

Physical recovery is visible tubes, reports, scars, but the emotional impact? That is harder to measure. I faced anxiety, fear of recurrence and guilt over past habits. Sometimes even anger -"Why me?"

So, we sought help. Not just from cardiologists, but from a therapist.

- Weekly sessions helped me process the trauma.
- Journaling gave me thoughts of a safe space.
- Guided meditation helped calm the mental chatter.

Healing became **multi-dimensional** - heart, body, mind and devotion.

Embracing Slowness in a Fast World

Speed had once defined his identity- how fast I replied to emails, closed bugs, solved escalations.

But now, **slowness has become strong**.

- Slow meals.

- Slow walks after dinner.

- Even slow conversations, where I *listened* more than he spoke.

In a world wired for hustle, slowness is radical. But it gave me something I never had before: **presence**.

Redefining Success

Success used to mean promotions, bonuses, and visibility.

Now, success looks like this:

- Waking up without fatigue.

- Completing eight thousand steps before lunch.

- Laughing freely with our kids over dinner.

- Finishing a week without pain or panic.

It is not that I stopped being ambitious, but he began redefining ambition from climbing ladders to building balance, from earning more to living. better.

Community and Connection: Sharing Story

I never planned to talk about what happened.

It felt personal, private, even shameful at first.

But silence helps no one.

Eventually, I opened with the colleagues, friends, even on LinkedIn connections.

The response was overwhelming.

- Others in their forties shared their own near misses.
- Younger peers thanked him for encouraging checkups.
- Teams began adopting heart-healthy practices together.

My story became a **beacon**. Not for sympathy, but for **awareness**.

When you tell the truth, others find theirs.

Living With Intention: A New Philosophy

Intentional living is not reaching perfection. It is alignment. Every choice I make now is filtered through one question:

"Will this support my health, my joy, and my peace?"

Not always, of course. The days are still hard, the habits are still tempting, but the direction is clear.

- Intentional work.
- Intentional rest.
- Intentional food, movement.
- relationships.

It is not about fear of another attack.

It is about honoring the life he almost lost.

6. Final Words: For Every IT Professional Out There

If you are reading this and you are:

- Tired all the time.
- Skipping meals.
- Trading health for targets.
- Dismissing chest pain as acidity.
- Telling yourself "It won't happen to me."

Please – Pause...

Because it can happen. It nearly happened to us. And it does not take a massive change, just a *decisive* one.

- Live with awareness.
- Live with boundaries.
- Live with joy, movement, and rest.
- Live like your heart matters - because it does.

This is not just his story. This could be yours.

Let it have a different ending.

7. A Second Chance: A New Purpose

Recovery is not just about regaining health; it is about reimagining life.

After five months of focused healing both physical and emotional, I gradually returned to my corporate routine. The same office chair, the same Teams meetings, the same systems, and stakeholders. But something fundamental had changed.

I had changed.

I no longer lived on an autopilot. Every meeting I had with stakeholders was now balanced with mindfulness. Every deadline honored with discipline, but not at the cost of my well-being. I built habits around walking, deep breathing, timely meals, and mental rest. And for three more years, I gave my best to my career, this time without giving away his soul.

But then, something stirred within him an itch I could no longer ignore.

"If I was given a second life," then maybe it is time to live a second dream." The purpose of life.

And with that, I made the boldest decision of all. **I left the corporate world behind.**

Not out of defeat, but with grace and intention. I embraced a new identity one that always lingered in the background, waiting to be awake I decided to become a **writer, a thinker, a creator.**

Today, I have authored **three books** in the fields of Information Industry as below:

- **Artificial Intelligence: An In-depth Introduction.**

- **Cloud Migration: The Definitive Guide.**
- **Demystifying AWS - Unleash the Power of the Cloud.**

I am also currently serving on the Non-Executive Advisory Boards of select startups, providing strategic guidance and mentorship.

Above work of mine are long-time areas of expertise. I continue to inspire readers across the country and am currently working on my next book series.

My story is not just about surviving a heart attack. It is about finding clarity through crisis. It is about turning pain into purpose. It is about discovering that sometimes, the greatest breakthroughs come disguised as breakdowns.

And to anyone out there still stuck in the blur of busyness, chasing deadlines with a tired heart, here is our message:

"Life may not give you a second chance. But if it does - do not just return to who you were. Become who you were meant to be."

8. After the Fall: What We Learned

Surviving a cardiac arrest is like giving me a second life and with it comes a profound understanding of what truly matters. As I sit back and reflect on my journey, I can identify a handful of valuable lessons that have reshaped the way I live, think, and prioritize.

Health Not Optional

Before this incident, I often took my health for granted. I ignored warning signs, attributed chest pain and nausea to acidity, and delayed checkups. Now, I realize the body always speaks we just must listen. A slight discomfort can sometimes be a life-threatening sign. The greatest wealth truly is health.

Never Ignore Symptoms

The earliest lesson I learnt came in the form of chest tightness, unusual fatigue, and nausea. For days I dismissed them, thinking they were minor digestive issues. But heart attacks often present subtly, especially in men around my age. If I had gone to the hospital earlier for regular checkups, the journey would not have been so severe. Prompt action saves lives.

Family is your Greatest Strength

Through every test, procedure, and sleepless night, my wife and children stood by me. They became my caretakers, my emotional anchors, and my source of hope. Their love gave me the strength to fight even when my body was failing. I learned that healing is not just physically, it's deeply emotional.

Faith as a Form of Medicine

The **Maha Mrityunjay**, a Mantra became my daily ritual. Its rhythm calmed me; its power gave me courage. Faith did not replace medicine, but it became the silent partner in my recovery. It brought purpose to my pain and strength to my soul.

Believe in God and The Power of Meditation

Trust in a higher power gave me the emotional strength to endure the most difficult days of my life. Meditation helped me control my fear, reduce anxiety, and stay grounded. In moments when the future seemed uncertain, prayer and mindfulness became my anchor. This spiritual discipline transformed my mindset, helping me embrace calm over chaos.

Simplicity Underrated

After returning home, the simplest things brought the most joy sunlight on my face, the sound of my children laughing, the smell of home cooked food. I no longer seek elaborate events or expensive outings. My world exists in the daily details of life.

Physical Movement is Healing

Starting with ten steps a day, I built my strength back one walk at a time. Today, I walk 6,000 steps a day. Movement, however small, is medicine for the heart, mind, and spirit.

Stress A Silent Killer

I have learned to say no, to pause, and to disconnect from chaos. Deadlines no longer define me. Stress can be more harmful to your health than smoking or drinking. Chronic stress affects the heart, weakens the immune system, and disrupts mental well-being. Unlike occasional habits, ongoing stress silently damages the body over time, making it a serious and often overlooked threat to long-term health and longevity.

Laughter Therapeutic

We laughed, even though the pain about my food hallucinations, my whispered jokes, and our shared silences. Humor carried us forward when strength alone was not enough.

New life - New Habits

Post-recovery, my diet, schedule, and mindset have changed completely. I eat better, sleep deeper, and live slower. I value wellness over work, purpose over pace.

Every Moment as a Blessing

I learned that life is fragile, and each breath is a gift. I cherish every sunrise, every prayer, every hug, and every heartbeat. I no longer chase tomorrow I live today.

These lessons are not just mine they are for anyone who has given a second chance or hopes to avoid needing one. Let them guide your days. Let them soften your pace. Let them remind you. Life is not just about surviving. It is about truly living.

Part-III Five Beats to Heart Healing (5D): Data, Diagnostics, Diet, Devotion, Dedication

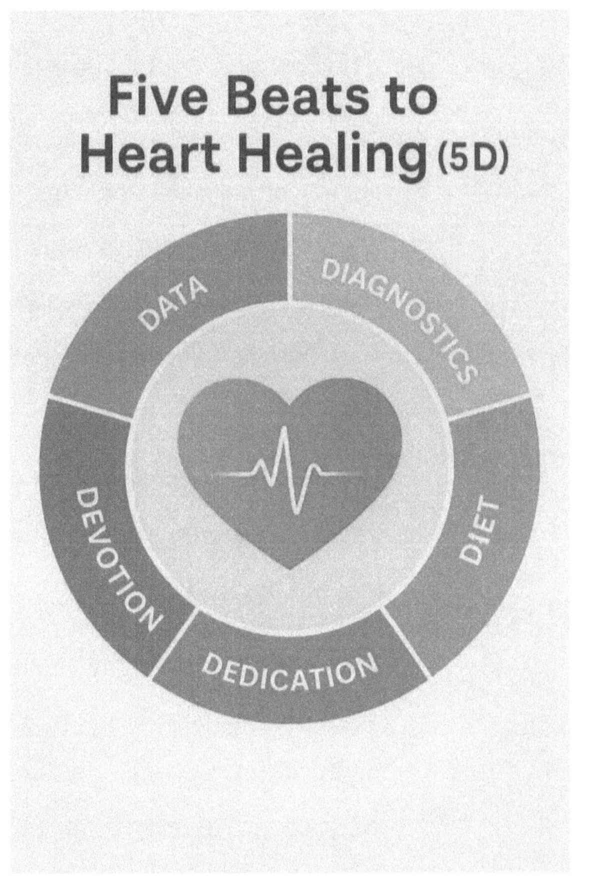

1. The Mathematical Triggers: What the Data Reveals

After the storm had passed, we left with countless questions: *Why did it happen? Was it sudden or silently building up? Could we have known in advance?* The search for answers led us deep into the world of health data. We discovered something that gave us clarity the numbers behind heart attacks.

Heart attacks rarely "just happen." The warning signs are always there in your medical reports, your lifestyle patterns, and your body's quiet signals. Most of us just do not look.

The data does not lie. And if we learn to read it, we can rewrite our stories before they turn into emergencies.

To understand why my husband, a middle-aged professional in his late 40s, suffered a heart attack and subsequent cardiac arrest, we turn to a crucial resource: **Data**. The dataset from Kaggle "Heart Attack Cases in India" is not just a table of medical records, it reflects the hidden dangers lurking behind sedentary jobs, poor lifestyle choices, and neglected health.

Let us unpack what the numbers reveal. Let us walk through what we find and how it applies directly to professionals like him, city bound, stressed, and living with the illusion of youth and time.

1. The High-Risk Age Window

The dataset includes individuals ranging from their 30s to 80s. But a strong concentration of **heart attack cases appears between the ages of 40s and 60s**, which aligns with the age of my husband when he suffered his cardiac event. In our modern day corporate culture, this age group represents professionals in mid-to-senior roles, often shouldering the heaviest workload and responsibilities.

Insight:

The patients who had heart attacks were aged **44–58**. This "danger decade" overlaps with the period when people often ignore annual check-ups, dismiss chest discomfort, and assume fatigue is just "part of the job."

2. Blood Pressure - The Quiet Alarm

Blood pressure is one of the most significant indicators. The dataset contains two critical fields:

- **BP_Systolic (upper number)**
- **BP_Diastolic (lower number)**

Ideal blood pressure should be around **120/80**, but in a few heart attack cases, systolic values range from **140 to 180**, and diastolic values creep above **90**, indicating **stage 1 or 2 hypertension** a dangerous zone.

Why it matters:

Sustained high pressure damages artery walls, leading to plaque buildup (atherosclerosis), which narrows or blocks coronary arteries, triggering a heart attack.

3. Cholesterol - The Blockade Builder

Another major player is **Cholesterol Level.** According to the dataset, individuals who had heart attacks frequently had cholesterol values exceeding **200 mg/dL**, it is even going beyond **230**.

Typical pattern in dataset:

- **Normal patients**: Cholesterol ~ 170 - 190
- **Heart attack patients**: Cholesterol ~ 210–250

This reinforces the direct link between **bad cholesterol (LDL)** and artery clogging. High cholesterol narrows arteries, restricting oxygen flow and leading to myocardial infarction (heart attack).

4. Diabetes and Blood Sugar - The Hidden Factor

The dataset's **Blood Sugar** field provides another layer. Few individuals with heart attacks had fasting sugar levels above **120 mg/dL**, indicating **prediabetes or diabetes**. Diabetes doubles the risk of heart disease due to its impact on blood vessels and inflammation.

In our case:

My husband had fluctuating sugar levels.

Although he was not formally diabetic, stress-induced sugar spikes played a role in a phenomenon increasingly common in IT professionals.

5. Smoking - A Modifiable Culprit

The **Smoking** column in the dataset is telling. Although not every heart attack patient smoked, **a sizable portion of affected individuals were mild or regular smokers**.

My husband fell into this category - a mild smoker, social, not regular, but enough to accumulate risk over time. Even occasional smoking narrows arteries and affects oxygen transport in the blood.

6. Family History - Not Always the Case

Interestingly, **Family History** was not present in every case. My husband had **no direct family history** of heart ailments. A common misconception is that if your parents did not have heart issues, you are safe.

Data says otherwise:

Data reveals that **40–45%** of heart attack

patients had **no family history**, proving that **lifestyle and health markers matter more** than genetics alone.

7. Sedentary Lifestyle and Exercise Level

In the dataset, **Exercise Level** was marked as *Low* in a sizable number of heart attack cases. Desk jobs, long hours, and skipped gym plans are not just lifestyle issues - they are **predictors of cardiovascular risk**.

A 30-minute walk can help, but many patients reported "Low" or "No" exercise activity - and my husband was one of them, stuck between deadlines and late meetings.

8. The Red Flags - ECG and Heart Rate

The parameters **Heartrate** and the **ECG result** provide additional insights:

- Many affected individuals had **resting heart rates over one hundred**, even while sedentary - a sign of underlying stress or cardiovascular strain.

- **Abnormal ECG results** were present in pre-attack check-ups for several patients in the dataset.

These metrics should not be ignored. Regular health screening with ECG and monitoring resting heart rate can help detect early signs of trouble.

The story behind each row in the dataset is personal - and one of those rows could have been my husband. The numbers tell a grim but necessary truth: heart attacks are often the **culmination of years of ignored signs**, not sudden shocks.

Through this section, we have learned:

- Which **factors matter most**: Age, blood pressure, cholesterol, diabetes, smoking, sedentary lifestyle.

- Why **monitoring data saves lives**: Predictive tools based on these parameters could help flag high-risk individuals well before disaster strikes.

In the next section, we'll go deeper showing how to **use these parameters in real life** to create a predictive model using simple tools (like Excel or a machine learning app), helping people stay one step ahead.

2. Predicting and Preventing with Data: Driven Diagnostics

What if my husband's cardiac arrest could have been foreseen? What if a simple tool-based on his age, cholesterol, blood pressure, and other vital signs could have warned us before it was too late?

That is not just a dream. Thanks to the increasing availability of health data and machine learning tools, **predictive healthcare is now a reality**, and it can be explained in a way that everyone can understand even without a medical or technical background.

1. From Symptoms to Signals - Making Sense of Health Data

Let us revisit the data fields that matter most:

Key Indicator	Meaning
Age	Older age increases risk, especially > 45 for men
Cholesterol_Level	Higher cholesterol = more plaque in arteries
BP_Systolic/Diastolic	High blood pressure stresses the heart
Blood_Sugar	Diabetes or prediabetes accelerate heart disease
Heart_Rate	Elevated rates (resting >100 bpm) signal potential strain
Smoking	Constricts blood vessels and increases clot risk
Diabetes / Obesity	Both lead to vascular damage and chronic inflammation
Exercise_Level	Low activity means poor heart conditioning

Key Indicator	Meaning
ECG_Result	Abnormal readings often precede heart events
Family_History	Adds background risk, even if other metrics seem fine
Heart_Attack	The actual target we want to predict (Yes/No)

These parameters collectively determine risk. In my husband's case, although he was a mild smoker and had no family history, the combination of high stress, slightly elevated cholesterol, and low exercise created a perfect storm.

2. Building a Simple Heart Risk Predictor

You do not need to be a data scientist to build a predictor. Even using tools like **Excel** or **Google Sheets**, people can create a **scoring system** to assess their own risk. Here is how:

Step 1: Assign a Risk Score for Each Variable

Parameter	Risk Threshold	Score
Age > 45	Yes	+1
Cholesterol > 200	Yes	+2
Systolic BP > 140	Yes	+2
Diastolic BP > 90	Yes	+1
Blood Sugar > 120	Yes	+1
Heart Rate > 100	Yes	+1
Smoker	Yes	+1
Diabetes	Yes	+1
Obesity	Yes	+1
No Exercise	Yes	+2
Abnormal ECG	Yes	+2

Total Score: 0 to 15

- **0–4**: Low Risk
- **5–9**: Moderate Risk
- **10–15**: High Risk (Consult a cardiologist immediately)

My Husband's Example:

Parameter	Value	Risk?	Score
Age	47	☑	1
Cholesterol	~203	☑	2
BP Systolic	~145	☑	2
BP Diastolic	~85	✗	0
Blood Sugar	~117	✗	0
Heart Rate	~112	☑	1
Smoker	Mild	☑	1
Diabetes	No	✗	0
Obesity	No	✗	0
Exercise	Low	☑	2
ECG	Abnormal	☑	2

Total Score = 11 (High Risk)

Had we done this scoring even a month earlier, we might have been alert.

3. Machine Learning for Everyone - Simplified

While manual scoring is useful, machine learning takes it a step further. By feeding this dataset into a predictive model, like **Logistic Regression** or **Random Forest**, we can create a digital assistant that learns from past cases to assess new ones.

Here's what happens behind the scenes:

- The model analyzes **patterns** in thousands of patients.
- It learns that, say, **high BP + smoking + abnormal ECG** is a red flag.
- When given a new profile (like my husband's), it outputs a **probability score** of heart attack risk (e.g., 84% chance).

There are even **open-source tools and no-code platforms** like:

- Teachable Machine by Google
- KNIME

- IBM Watson Studio Lite
- Microsoft Azure ML Designer

You need to simply:

a) Upload the dataset.
b) Select "Heart_Attack" as the outcome.
c) Choose input variables.
d) Click "Train Model".
e) Assess your own profile.

4. Predictive Healthcare at Home

Imagine an app that combines this logic:

- You input basic health stats.
- It alerts you if you are in the red zone.
- It recommends a doctor visit, diet changes, or stress relief.

That is the future we are heading toward, and, in many ways, it is already here.

5. Final Words - Prevention Is Possible

Numbers told us what our bodies did not, my husband's heart attack was not random. It was predictable, even preventable with data.

So, this section is not just about modeling and algorithms. It is about empowering every professional, especially in high-stress tech environments, to take control of their health using everyday tools.

If you are reading this and fit the profile, you are overworked, over-caffeinated, under-exercised - start tracking your numbers today. Your body has a voice. Data helps you hear it.

3. Healing Inside Out: The Power of Diet

As we sat in the doctor's office during his discharge briefing, the cardiologist a seasoned professional with kind eyes and a firm voice leaned in and said, "If you want to not just survive but thrive, you must treat food as your first medicine."

That was our wake-up call.

In the world of IT where my husband worked, precision, systems, and processes ruled.

Now, we would bring that same precision to our meals. We were not looking for a crash diet or a short-term fix. This had to be a permanent, sustainable lifestyle transformation. Food had to become not just nourishment, but *therapy*.

The day he came home from the hospital, everything felt different.

Not just the way he walked slowly, carefully, with short breaths - but the way we both looked at life. Each step he took into the house felt like a gift. A few days earlier, we were not sure he would ever walk through that door again. A massive heart attack. A sudden cardiac arrest. A miraculous survival. And now, here we were - back home, but forever changed.

The home that once echoed with hurried mornings, late-night work calls, and weekend movie plans had now turned into a place of quiet observation and cautious movements. The bedroom became a mini recovery ward. A digital BP monitor sat on the side table, medication schedules were pinned on the fridge, and his side of the bed was artfully arranged with extra pillows to help him sleep upright.

But recovery was not just about medication, rest, or follow-up appointments. It was about what we did every single day from the moment he opened his eyes, to the meals he ate, to the energy that slowly returned to his tired body.

And that is when I realized: **healing had to begin in the kitchen.**

The same kitchen that once whipped up quick meals between Zoom calls was now our center of transformation. Every ingredient I picked, every dish I prepared, carried a weight of responsibility. It was not just about taste anymore, it was about life, about preventing another emergency, about reversing the damage that had done.

In those early days of home recovery, food quietly took center stage. I began reading, researching, talking to nutritionists, watching videos on heart-healthy diets. What I discovered was both simple and profound: **food could be his medicine.**

We began eliminating the harmful comforts rich curries, fried snacks, processed foods and started embracing a new kind of nourishment. Warm vegetable soups. Lightly sautéed greens. Fresh fruits. Whole grains. Hydrating herbal teas. Small, frequent meals that were gentle on his heart yet filled with healing nutrients.

At first, it felt restrictive. But soon, we found rhythm and meaning in these changes. Cooking became my quiet act of care. Eating became his daily dose of therapy.

We did not call it a "**diet**." It was not about counting calories or cutting carbs. It was about honoring his second chance. About choosing foods that reduced inflammation, lowered cholesterol, stabilized his blood pressure, and gave him strength.

Day by day, bit by bit, I could see the difference. His energy returned. His sleep improved. His fear began to lift. And with every balanced plate we shared at the dining table, our hope grew stronger.

Deconstructing Our Old Plate

Our journey began with unlearning.

We looked at our regular meals, those quick, after-work dinners and weekend indulgences, and started asking tough questions. Was that buttery paratha helping his arteries? Was the weekend mutton curry adding joy or jeopardy?

The answer was clear.

So, we started with **removal**. It was painful at first, emotionally more than physically. These foods were not just ingredients, they were part of our habits, our culture, our comfort.

What We Let Go:

- **Red and Processed Meats**: Goodbye to kebabs, sausages, and even our weekend biryani rituals. Studies showed these were laden with saturated fats and cholesterol.

- **Fried Foods**: Out went the samosas, pakoras, and restaurant Chinese food dripping with oil.
- **Refined Grains and Sugars**: We cleared the pantry of white bread, processed food, sugar-laden biscuits, and sweets.
- **Full-fat Dairy**: No more extra ghee-laced rotis or creamy desserts. Cheese and butter replaced with heart-friendly oils.

It was not easy. But every item we removed felt like a load lifted off his heart literally and metaphorically.

Rebuilding Our Plate with Purpose

With the old diet stripped away, we had a blank canvas. And on it, we began painting a new picture of health and healing.

What We Embraced:

1. **Whole Plant-Based Foods**

   Our meals became colorful. Spinach, broccoli, beetroot, carrots, okra, raw papaya, capsicum, and sweet potatoes. Our kitchen turned into a mini farm.

2. **Whole Grains Over Refined Grains**

   We discovered the joy of **millets** like flax seeds, oatmeal, and avocado. Brown rice is replaced with white weekly once in a while. We chose the whole wheat flour carefully, ensuring this not refined.

3. **Legumes and Lentils**

   Whole Moong dal, Chana, Rajma, Toor dal - these became our primary sources of protein. High in fiber, they kept his cholesterol in check and energy stable.

4. **Fruits for Natural Sweetness**

   Berries, bananas, apples, papaya, guava, and oranges became his daily treat. A bowl of fruits with honey and black pepper, instead of a biscuit or namkeen, became his tea-time joy.

5. **Nuts and Seeds in Moderation**

   A handfuls of almonds, walnuts, raisins, figs and blue berries found our way into breakfast bowls and smoothies. Rich in omega-3s, they offered heart-protective benefits.

6. **Healthy Oils and Fats**

   We used mustard oil, rice bran or sunflower oil in lesser amounts for cooking, but more importantly, we *reduced* oil usage drastically.

7. **Boiled Chicken and eggs**

   Boiled chicken and eggs support heart health by providing lean protein, essential for muscle repair and maintaining heart function. When consumed in moderation, they help manage cholesterol levels and promote overall cardiovascular well-being.

A New Way of Cuisine

This was not just about new ingredients; it was about **rethinking cooking** itself.

- We started **boiling, steaming, baking, sautéing** instead of deep-frying.

- We explored **plant-based recipes** inspired by Mediterranean and Indian cuisines.

- Herbs and spices like **turmeric, cumin, coriander, cinnamon, ginger** and **garlic** added depth and healing.

- We cooked in **smaller portions**, ate slowly, and stopped when full.

- At home, we prepared traditional religious dishes meals woven into the fabric of our **childhood**, lovingly prepared by our mother. These time-honored foods bring not only nourishment and comfort but also a deep sense of spiritual fulfillment.

- We should approach our meals with a positive mindset, avoiding negative remarks like 'this doesn't taste good,' 'there's less salt,' or 'it's not tasty,' as such thoughts can bring negative energy into our body and affect our health. It's also important to stay away from gadgets while eating, so we can be fully present and mindful during our meals.

A Sample Day food on Our New Plate

MORNING

- Warm lemon water or lemon tea.
- Suii upma or Dosa/Idly with makhana (lotus seeds), and walnuts

MID-MORNING SNACK

- A bowl of banana/papaya/ apple slices

LUNCH

- White/Brown rice with moong dal, cooked carrot/ beans vegetables
- Cucumber and tomato salad with a dash of lemon and black pepper powder

EVENING

- Herbal tea with roasted chickpeas or a small fruit smoothie

DINNER

- Chapati/Millet khichdi with vegetables and turmeric
- Side of sautéed mushrooms with black pepper

Science Behind Simplicity

What we were doing was not random. It was backed by science. I read late into the night books, medical journals, even case studies.

- **Dr. Dean Ornish** had shown heart disease could be reversed through a low-fat, vegetarian diet combined with stress management and exercise.
- **Dr. Caldwell Esselstyn** had similar outcomes with a strict plant-based, oil-free diet.
- These approaches not only stabilized heart disease but even showed signs of reversal in plaque buildup.

Food was not just support; it was frontline medicine.

The Emotional Journey of Food

Food is deeply emotional. It is celebration, comfort, and culture. We faced resistance from ourselves, from friends, from extended family.

"Just one bite won't hurt," they would say.

But we stood our ground, not out of fear, but from a place of **respect for life**. He had gotten a second chance not everyone gets that. We would not waste it on short-lived pleasures.

Instead, we learned to **celebrate differently**. Festivals with fruit-based desserts, potlucks with millet upma and hummus, birthdays with avocado chocolate mousse.

Food brought us together, now in a healthier way.

The Results – Beyond the Numbers

In six months:

- His **LDL (bad cholesterol)** dropped.
- His **HDL (good cholesterol)** went up.
- He lost over ten kilos of weight without trying to "diet."
- His **blood pressure** stabilized.
- He had more **energy** and **mental clarity** than ever before.

But more than physical, the emotional and spiritual transformation was profound. There was less fear. More gratitude. A renewed zest for life.

A Heart's Second Chance: Our Journey of Faith

was less fear. More gratitude. A renewed zest for life.

4. Beyond Science: The Power of Devotion

1. The Pause Between Heartbeats

There are moments in life when time does not just slow, it stops. The day my husband collapsed from a sudden heart attack, followed by a cardiac arrest, our world came to a screeching halt. In the ICU, surrounded by machines, sterile walls, and the unblinking gaze of monitors, medicine did its part. Doctors worked relentlessly. Protocols were followed, but as hours turned into an eternal wait and his status lingered between uncertainty and hope, something beyond science stepped in **our faith**.

We are not blindly religious people. Like many modern Indian families, we balanced logic with tradition, rituals with rationality. But in that darkest moment, when even the best medical intervention had reached its threshold, we instinctively turned to the divine not out of fear, but from an inner conviction we did not even know we carried.

2. The Chant That Filled the Silence

As the news spread among close family and friends, something incredible began happening. Our home, which just hours ago was echoing with panic and silence, was now alive with the sound of a powerful prayer. The **Mahamrityunjaya Mantra**, also known as the death-conquering chant of Lord Shiva, began to echo continuously softly, reverently from a small speaker in our prayer room.

"ॐ त्र्यम्बकं यजामहे सुगन्धिं पुष्टिवर्धनम्।
उर्वारुकमिव बन्धनान् मृत्योर्मुक्षीय मामृतात्॥ "

"Om Tryambakam Yajamahe Sugandhim Pushtivardhanam /

Urvarukamiva Bandhanan Mrityor Mukshiya Maamritat // "

Meaning:

We worship the three-eyed Lord Shiva, who permeates and nourishes all life and is fragrant like a blossoming flower. Just as a ripe cucumber naturally detaches from its stem, may we be liberated from the *bondage of death—**but not from immortality (spiritual liberation).***

अर्थ (भावार्थ):

हम त्रिनेत्र वाले भगवान शिव की पूजा करते हैं, जो जीवन को सुगंधित करते हैं और पोषण प्रदान करते हैं। जैसे खीरा (या बेल) पककर बिना किसी कष्ट के डंठल से अलग हो जाता है, वैसे ही हे प्रभु, हमें मृत्यु के बंधन से मुक्त करें, लेकिन अमरत्व (आध्यात्मिक अमरता) से नहीं।

We did not just play it for a few minutes. It ran **non-stop**, a 24-hour cycle of vibration and devotion. Each time it played, it felt like we were wrapping him in a blanket of spiritual strength. Even though he lay unconscious, we believed the vibrations of that sacred sound could reach his soul, could speak to the part of him that medicine could not touch.

There were moments when his vital dipped, his condition fluctuated and yet, the mantra continued. An anchor in a stormy sea. The chant was not a replacement for medical care, but a **companion to it**, a force that held him as doctors saved him.

3. Guided by the Wise: Rituals Rooted in Faith

In the hours that followed, we reached out not just to medical experts but also to **spiritual scholars and respected pandits**. We did not seek superstitions or easy assurances. We sought **guidance rooted in scriptural wisdom**.

A senior scholar we trusted told us gently, "You have done what needs to be done medically. Now offer the rest to the divine. Faith begins where control ends."

Following their advice, we performed **specific rituals**, not out of fear but with devotion. Each one was performed with clarity and intention lighting of ghee lamps, chanting of specific shlokas, and a Sankalp (sacred vow) for his well-being. These were not about rituals for ritual's sake, they were about **connecting our human fragility to a greater divine rhythm.**

4. Across Oceans, A Prayer was Heard

What moved us even more was how our circle of loved ones extended across borders and still stood by us, spiritually.

A dear friend of mine got in touch with her friend in **Germany**, a healer and spiritual practitioner, immediately began **distance healing sessions**. Each evening, as we sat in quiet prayer at home, she would enter a meditative state thousands of miles away, sending healing energy toward him. Skeptics might question such practices, but for us, every gesture of love and energy mattered. Every stream of positive intention felt like another thread holding him to life.

We began to realize *prayer, when done with faith, knows no boundaries. Not of distance, not of religion, not of doubt.*

5. A Center of Stillness Amidst Chaos

In the heart of Bengaluru, at the **Art of Living International Center**, one of our close family friends took his name and placed it before the divine altar. Special prayers were offered. In the peaceful energy of the center's meditation halls, chants were dedicated to his recovery. Though we could not be there in person, we felt the vibrations reaching us.

AOL had always emphasized **inner peace, breathing techniques, and connection with the higher self**. It reminded us that recovery was not only physical, but it was also emotional, mental, and spiritual. This was not just about surviving an illness. It was about emerging from it transformed.

6. Back Home, Rebirth and Fire

Weeks later, when he finally returned home, there were no grand celebrations due to the Covid pandemic. Just gratitude.

We arranged a **special Havan,** a sacred fire ceremony in our living room. The fire flickered gently, illuminating the faces of our family, who sat around in silent reverence. As the priest chanted verses invoking protection, healing, and renewal, we offered hawan samagri (sacred materials), ghee, and our deepest prayers into the flames.

That fire became symbolic. Of purification. Of surrender. Of new beginnings.

It was not about impressing any god or seeking divine favors. It was about aligning ourselves with something greater, something eternal. About acknowledging that **we do not control everything**, and yet, **we are not helpless either.**

7. Meditation: The Inner Retreat

As days passed and life slowly returned to a new rhythm, **meditation became his medicine.** It was not always easy, his mind would wander, his body still healing, breath shallow. But with practice, he found moments of stillness.

Each morning, he would sit by the window, eyes closed, focusing on his breath. Sometimes chanting softly, sometimes just observing in silence. We practiced simple **guided meditation**, visualizations of healing light, and gratitude reflections.

What medication did for the heart, meditation did for the mind. It reduced anxiety. It improved his sleep. It brought back confidence, slowly and surely.

8. Faith, Not Blindness

One might say this was all coincidence. That medicine alone saved him. But we know the full story. It was not either/or. It was **both**. Science worked outside. **Faith worked within.**

Our belief in God, in the teachings of Sanatana Dharma, did not emerge from blind adherence. It was built over the years, rooted in tradition, logic, and lived experience. We did not reject medical science, but we embraced fully. But when it reached its limit, we leaned into our **trust in the divine**.

And we were not alone. So many people came together not just physically, but spiritually lifted him up in prayer, in chanting, in silent intentions. The web of faith held him when the thread of life was thin.

5. Dedication from Friends and Support: Bound by Love

1. Alone, Yet Not Alone

The city was silent, gripped in the stillness of the Covid 19 lockdown. Roads deserted. Doors hut. Everyone was behind the walls safe, cautious, distant. And yet, at the exact moment when our family needed the world the most, a beautiful truth began to unfold **we were never truly alone**.

My husband, my life partner, a vibrant IT professional in his late forties, had just suffered a heart attack followed by a cardiac arrest. Everything happened in a terrifying instant. One moment he was with us, and the next, we were in the hospital, fighting for his life. During such a deeply personal and painful time, the pandemic made everything ten times harder. Most of our **relatives could not travel** due to restrictions and they had their own reasons not to travel due to their own family commitments. Airports closed. Borders sealed. But despite the physical absence, their **emotional presence surrounded us like a protective shield**.

Calls poured in. Messages of hope. Daily check-ins. Spiritual support. My phone never stopped ringing, and every word on the other end felt like a hand reaching out to hold mine, steadying me when my world shook. Every discussion, every prayer, every voice mattered.

2. The Hands That Lifted Us - Next Door Angels

While our extended family supported us from afar on virtual video call, our apartment community and nearby friends became our lifeline. When time was of the essence and fear had paralyzed me, it was a close friend and neighbor who sprang into action. Without hesitation, he drove my husband to the emergency room, weaving through the empty roads of a locked city with urgency and calm. He stayed with him as the doctors took over and ensured that proper medical care began immediately. In those crucial moments, he was more than a friend he was my strength.

In the days that followed, as I remained in the hospital corridor navigating reports, consulting doctors, handling insurance paperwork, and waiting endlessly, a few dear friends became my backbone. They didn't ask what needed to be done, they simply stepped in. With practical minds and grounded emotions, they spoke to doctors with clarity, helped me make decisions when my thoughts were clouded, and ensured I had food, water, and moments of rest. A medically trained friend patiently explained terms I could not comprehend and guided me through the overwhelming medical process.

Back at home, when I could not be there, our neighbors made sure our children were cared for. Food was arranged. Groceries appeared at the doorstep through online stores. I never had to ask if it all came with love. In a time when everyone was socially distant, our neighborhood stood close.

3. Rituals, Faith, and Friendships

As our family turned to faith during this crisis, the support from friends continued in beautiful, unexpected ways.

Following advice from spiritual scholars and family elders, we had to perform **specific rituals** for his recovery. But how would I manage them from the hospital, especially with the lockdown restrictions?

That is when **one of my neighbor's spouses** came in quietly. With devotion and grace, she managed the puja logistics, ensuring that each ritual was performed correctly. It was an act of true friendship, stepping into sacred space on our behalf when we could not.

Meanwhile, a close family friend, who was associated with a spiritual foundation (Art of Living), organized a special healing session at the center in Bengaluru. In a time when science and prayer stood side by side, her quiet act of devotion meant the world to us. She chanted. She meditated. She prayed for healing energy to reach my husband, and I believe it did.

4. Bonds That Never Break- The NIT Brotherhood

Some friendships are forged in college and only grow stronger with time. Our **NIT (National Information Technology) Raipur batchmates** became an invisible, yet powerful, circle of strength around us.

Despite being scattered across India and abroad few in the US, others in different corners of the country they were all **just a call away**. Daily calls turned into group discussions. Friends connected us with **leading doctors from India and the United States**, reviewing reports, offering second opinions, and providing clarity when things felt confusing or frightening.

Beyond medical guidance, they brought emotional support humor when I was too afraid to smile, perspective when panic took over. Their faith in his recovery often steadied my wavering heart.

5. Around the Clock Compassion

While the days were overwhelming, the nights were the hardest, dark, silent, full of worry. That was when a few close friends became my nighttime support system. They didn't just check in once a day. They were always there, whether it was morning, noon, or midnight. One couple offered a quiet, grounding presence through phone and video calls, gently reminding me to breathe, to sleep, to eat. They helped me reconnect with my strength when I felt completely depleted. Another friend, with a calm voice and a patient ear, allowed me to cry, vent, or simply sit in silence. That quiet, unwavering friendship became an anchor in a storm I never saw coming.

6. The Quiet Heroes

In every crisis, there are heroes who do not wear capes but walk beside you, holding pieces of your broken world together. For us, these were our **friends and neighbors**, our **relatives miles away**, our **college family**, and our **spiritual companions**.

In a world that teaches us to be self-sufficient, this experience reminded us of something deeper: **we are meant to lean on each other,** and that learning is not a weakness, it's humanity.

When I look back now, I do not remember the beeping machines or the tense hospital corridors. I remember his urgency. His calm. His reliability. Her prayers. Their messages and strength. His listening. The endless voices from NIT Raipur. The distant prayers of relatives. The warm food left outside our door.

7. Gratitude Etched in Our Hearts

Today, my husband is walking again. Talks again. Smiles again. He may not remember every detail of those harrowing days, but I do. And I carry with me not just the trauma of those moments, but **the tremendous grace that surrounded us**.

We often speak of miracles in religious texts. But I have seen modern miracles in friendships, in support systems, in a community that showed up without being asked.

To each person who stood by us near or far, silently, or vocally we are forever grateful. Your love helped write the story of his survival.

Two Hundred Days Later...

Life had taken a beautiful turn! Mukesh was feeling so much healthier and stronger compared to those challenging days back in May 2020 when he faced a heart attack and cardiac arrest. Regular hospital visits for check-ups and medication adjustments have become a part of our journey toward wellness.

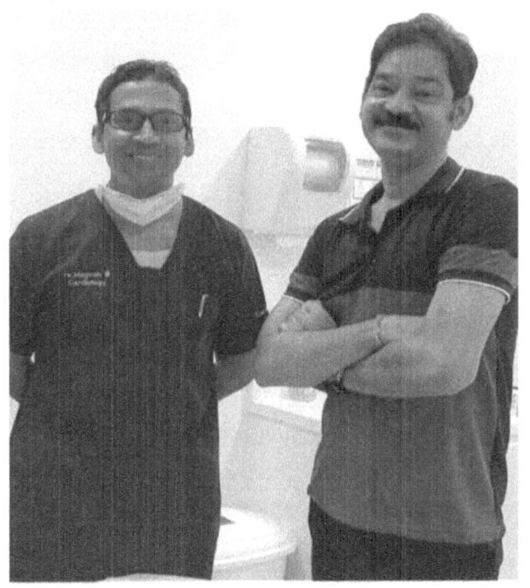

One special day, we captured a joyful moment with Dr. Magesh, the amazing cardiologist who guided us through it all. Mukesh was beaming with energy and confidence, a true picture of recovery. It felt wonderful to take a photo with the doctor who played such a vital role in his healing our heartfelt thanks will always be with him!

Acknowledgments

The writing of this novel *A Heart's Second Chance: Our Journey of Faith* has been an extremely a personal and emotional experience. This book is not just a reflection of a medical emergency, it is a testimony of love, faith, and the extraordinary strength of human connection.

First and foremost, I bow in gratitude to **God**, whose divine grace supported us through the darkest hours. It was his presence that gave me strength when mine shattered.

To my **beloved husband Mukesh**, this book exists because of his courage and willpower to come back. Your resilience, despite facing death **twice**, continues to inspire me every day.

A very special note of thanks to **Dr. Magesh Balakrishnan**, Consultant Interventional Cardiologist at Manipal Hospital, Sarjapur Road, Bangalore. Your timely intervention and compassionate care saved my husband's life for which I will remain forever grateful.

To the **ICU nurses, cardiology department, duty doctors, dietitians, physiotherapists**, and **support staff at Manipal Hospital**, you were our heroes during a period of fear and vulnerability.

To my **Dear kids**, your quiet strength, prayers, and trust gave me hope when I had none. You are the light that guided me through this storm.

To my **parents** and **in-laws** for their unwavering support from a distance, with special thanks to my **mother**, whose comforting words and constant presence even from a distance were a source of immense strength to me. I also extend my heartfelt appreciation to my **brother, brothers-in-law**, and **sister-in-law**, whose guidance and thoughtful counsel were invaluable in making critical decisions regarding his treatment.

To our **neighbors and friends**, who stepped in without hesitation, thank you for being our pillars when we needed you the most. You rushed to our side, accompanied my husband to the hospital, drove me back and forth, and offered strength without expecting anything in return.

To our **NIT** (National Institute of Technology, Raipur) circle of friends, based out all over the world in continued support.

To both of our office colleagues and distant healers across the globe who sent prayers, energy, and positivity this journey has shown us the profound power of collective faith.

This book is dedicated to all of you. You gave us a second chance in life, and this story would be incomplete without acknowledging your role in it.

A Heart's Second Chance

Life drifts like a fleeting tide,

Its course unknown, its fate untried.

Hold each laugh, each love, each day,

For time may steal them all away.

If life returns, a second chance,

Let joy be free, let hearts still dance.

No space for sorrow, nor regret,

Cherish the light before it sets.

When storms arise and shadows call,

Fear may whisper, doubts may fall.

Yet hope remains a guiding flame,

Strength is born when hearts proclaim.

Let courage rise, let fear subside,

For light will glow where faith resides.

No room for darkness, nor despair,

Determined souls will win the air.

Have faith in God, the guiding star,

Whose wisdom shapes the world afar.

Let kindness flow in words we weave,

A gentle touch, a heart to grieve.

No harm be done, no soul in pain,

Let love and mercy break the chain.

Walk righteously, with steps so true,

And grace shall lead the way anew.

Give with grace, expect no gain,

Let love flow like gentle rain.

A selfless heart will never stray,

Its light will guide the darkest way.

Recall the hands that stood so true,

Forget the ones who never knew.

Let wisdom guard where feelings sway,

A mind grown strong will never fray.